FIERY VISION

The Life and Death of John Brown

FIERY

The Life and De

VISION

h of John Brown

CLINTON COX

Scholastic Press   New York

PHOTO CREDITS

Pages 31, 39, 54, 119, 140, 184, 197: Brown Brothers, Sterling, PA; pages 90, 114, 123: Corbis-Bettmann; pages 60, 192: Culver Pictures; pages 2, 27, 97, 106, 153: The Granger Collection, New York; page 82: The Historical Society of Pennsylvania; page 74: Kansas State Historical Society, Topeka, Kansas; pages 62, 71: Library of Congress; pages 170-171: National Park Services; pages 35, 109, 144, 164, 179, 210, 213: New York Public Library; pages 12, 16, 51, 77, 132: Schomburg Center for Research in Black Culture; page 64: Sophia Smith Collection, Smith College; pages 7, 24, 44, 149, 159: West Virginia State Archives, Boyd B. Stutler Collection

LIBRARY OF CONGRESS CATALOGING-IN-PUBLICATION DATA

Cox, Clinton
Fiery Vision: The Life and Death of John Brown / by Clinton Cox
p.   cm.
Includes bibliographical references and index. Summary: A biography of the controversial abolitionist who led the raid on the United States arsenal at Harpers Ferry
ISBN 0-590-47574-6
[1. Brown, John, 1800-1859 — Juvenile literature. 2. Abolitionists-United States — Biography — Juvenile literature. [1. Abolitionists.]] I. Title.
E451.C88 1997
973.7′116′092—dc20   96-21368   CIP   AC
12 11 10 9 8 7 6 5 4 3 2 1
Printed in the U.S.A.   37
First printing, April 1997

Text set in Bembo 13/16
Book design by Marijka Kostiw

TABLE OF CONTENTS

PROLOGUE

This is the story of John Brown, whose raid on Harpers Ferry, Virginia, on the night of October 16, 1859, polarized the nation and helped propel it to the Civil War and the destruction of slavery.

Brown was one of the most controversial figures of his time, and his name continues to provoke both anger and admiration, though he was executed shortly after the raid.

Historians routinely use such words as "fanatic" and "murderer" to describe him, but use no such words to describe the slave owners and slavery supporters he fought. What is it about John Brown that continues to arouse such passion, when the cause for which he gave his life — the destruction of slavery — was achieved just a few years after his death?

It is as if both he and the issues he fought for are alive and still being contested today, and in a way they are. Brown's belief in the total equality of all people, a belief rare in his lifetime, is a concept that continues to divide this nation.

To understand John Brown, one must first understand slavery, for that is the force that shaped his life and the life of the nation he lived in.

When John Brown was born on May 9, 1800, there were approximately one million men, women, and children held in slavery in this country, but by the time he died in 1859 there were four million. The institution of slavery was upheld by the force of federal, state, and local governments, and no one was more violent than the slave owners and their supporters.

There were leaders who wanted to end slavery, but they were rare. Eleven of the country's first sixteen presidents were slave owners, as were a majority of its Supreme Court justices, attorney generals, and Speakers of the House of Representatives, from the birth of the nation to the Civil War.

When George Washington was commissioned a major in the Virginia militia at the age of nineteen, one of his first duties was to search slaves for weapons so they would not be able to fight for freedom.

The laws he helped enforce provided, among other harsh punishments, that "any slave caught off his master's plantation without a pass after dark shall be dismembered."

Escaped men, women, and children were often hunted down by vicious, specially trained "Negro dogs," and the punishment for escape attempts — or for any action that displeased a slaveowner — was whatever the slave owner desired. Black people could be killed for any reason or for no reason at all.

A British official visiting South Carolina said: "It is literally no more to kill a slave than to shoot a dog."

Ultimate acts of barbarity were inherent in a system that treated men, women, and children like cattle because of the color of their skin.

Historians are as susceptible to racial perceptions as anyone else, and one must wonder how much more sympathetically they would have treated John Brown if the slave owners he fought had been black and the slaves he fought to free had been white.

George Washington and Thomas Jefferson sometimes agonized over slavery because they knew it was morally indefensible and potentially destructive to the nation, but both used their political power to protect it.

The price of Southern membership in the United States was always Northern acceptance of slavery, and Southern leaders repeatedly threatened to secede and form their own nation if attempts were made to end slavery.

The threat of a violent clash over slavery was always just below the surface, even if few leaders dared publicly speak of it. John Quincy Adams, who publicly curried favor with politically powerful slave owners because he wanted to be president, privately approved the use of violence to end slavery even if it split the nation apart.

"If slavery is destined to be the sword in the hand of the destroying angel which is to sever the ties of this Union, the same sword will cut in sunder the bonds of slavery itself, . . ." he wrote in his diary, in words that would be echoed almost four decades later by John Brown: ". . . calamitous and desolating as this course of events in its progress must be, so glorious would be its final issue, that, as God shall judge me, I dare not say that it is not to be desired."

As John Brown grew to manhood, he watched while the growing nation threatened to tear itself apart over the monstrous contradiction that had been with it since its birth and protected by its Constitution: the celebration of both liberty and slavery.

In the last years of John Brown's life, the slave empire in the United States stretched from the Atlantic Ocean in the East to the Rio Grande in the West, from the Ohio River in the North to the Gulf of Mexico in the South. It was one of the largest and most brutal slave empires the world has ever known, and slaveholders were the country's single most powerful economic and political force.

It was as if the United States was a boat caught in the grip of two mighty opposing tides: one struggling to carry it forward to the light of liberty for all people regardless of color, the other whirling it backward to the darkness and cruelty of slavery.

The events of the time forced men and women to support or oppose slavery, whether they wanted to make a choice or not. It was against this background that John Brown lived his life and made his choices.

He stood at the center of the greatest crisis this country has ever known, and gave his life to try to solve it.

"I think I cannot now better serve the cause I love so much than to die for it," he said a few days before he was hanged for the attack on Harpers Ferry, "and in my death I may do more than in my life."

Over one hundred thirty-five years later — because of his uncompromising belief in racial equality — a biography of John Brown remains as much a story of our time as of his.

CHAPTER ONE

THE CAUSE I LOVE SO MUCH

The year John Brown was born, 1800, a deeply religious slave named Gabriel Prosser organized over one thousand black men to fight for freedom in Virginia. Prosser believed that, like Samson, he was meant by God to deliver his people even if it cost him his life.

He planned to seize the arsenal in Richmond, arm his followers, and begin the struggle against slavery. But the plot was betrayed and Prosser was hanged, along with several of his followers.

The slave conspiracy's implications for the future of the United States were not lost on Governor James Monroe, who dispatched troops to put down the slaves and who later became the nation's fifth president.

"Unhappily," he observed, "while this class of people exists among us, we can never count with certainty on its tranquil submission."

Just weeks before Monroe expressed the fear felt by so many other white Americans, a child was born who would also come to believe that God meant him to deliver the slaves. And, like Prosser, that belief would lead him to plan to seize an arsenal in Virginia and use its weapons to bring freedom to the slaves.

The child's name was John Brown, and he was born May 9, 1800, in Torrington, Connecticut, to a deeply religious, antislavery farming couple named Owen and Ruth Brown.

The era the new child was born into was one when talk of freedom, justice, and equality seemed

John Brown's birthplace at Torrington, Connecticut.

in the air people breathed and the water they drank. Both his grandfathers had fought in the American Revolution, and the nation they helped form had elected George Washington as its first president just eleven years before.

But though most black Americans were held in slavery, they believed the words about freedom also applied to them and they were as willing as anyone else to die for it. (Thousands of black Americans had, in fact, fought in the Revolutionary War.)

In addition to Prosser's failed revolt, the year of John Brown's birth was also the year that a black man named Denmark Vesey purchased his freedom, in Charleston, South Carolina, and began planning a huge slave uprising. It was also the year black revolutionary Nat Turner was born, a man whose bloody rebellion years later would fire John Brown's imagination with the possibility of arming slaves to fight for their freedom.

The new country had been founded by men who said they believed "that all men are created equal" and entitled to "Life, Liberty, and the Pursuit of Happiness," but almost one million black people were held in slavery in the fledgling democracy of five million.

"As it is," Jefferson said in describing his perception of the country's (and his own) moral dilemma in preaching freedom while practicing slavery, "we have the wolf by the ears, and we can neither hold him, or safely let him go. Justice is in one scale, and self-preservation in the other."

Most white Americans openly supported slavery or quietly accepted it, hoping it would one day die out on its own.

But Owen Brown's God was color-blind — as his son's would be — and the words about freedom, liberty, and equality that his father died for in the Revolutionary War were truths that guided Owen Brown's life.

He was appalled when a slave owning minister from Virginia visited a local church and told the congregation he had a right to do anything he wanted with his human "property," including separating and selling husband, wife, and children. Owen Brown could not imagine anyone claiming such a right over him, his wife Ruth, or their children, and so he could not imagine anyone claiming such a right over any other people, regardless of the color of their skin.

Owen, who was so devoted to his wife that he called his marriage to her "the beginning of my days," said that ever since hearing the slave owner's arguments about "his property" that day in the church, "I have been an Abolitionist . . . I know we are not loved by many."

John Brown was five years old when his father moved the family to the Western Reserve in what is now northeastern Ohio. It was then on the fringe of the fledgling United States: a vast primeval forest of almost four million acres, where Senecas, Chippewas, Onondagas, Oneidas, Mingoes, and Ottawas outnumbered the few hundred whites.

The trip from Connecticut to the Western Reserve was a magical journey for the curious child, and one he never forgot.

Sometimes John rode horseback or helped his adopted brother, eleven-year-old Levi Blakeslee, drive the family's cows. His mother usually rode in the ox-drawn covered wagon holding his baby brother, Oliver. The other family members were three-year-old Salmon and seven-year-old Anna.

Years later, Brown remembered how the travelers often "met with Rattle Snakes which were very large; & which some of the company generally managed to kill." At night, seated around the campfire or about to go to sleep, they frequently heard the howling of wolves or the prowling of "wild beasts" in the nearby forest.

The Brown family's journey was part of a general westward migration, as restless men and women hoped there was a better life waiting for them over the next hill or around the next bend in the road.

Many were also deeply religious and wanted to spread Christianity, build schools and churches, and do whatever they could to make life better for themselves and others.

"I came with a determination to help build up,

and be a help in the support of, religion and civil order," Owen Brown said of his move to the Western Reserve.

But that first year took all his strength just to ensure the family's survival. They settled in the township of Hudson, Ohio, which had been founded just six years before by Deacon David Hudson of Connecticut. There were only twenty or thirty families in the township's twenty-five square miles, most of them transplanted Connecticut settlers who shared a belief that slavery was wrong.

It was the end of July when the Brown family arrived, and though they worked as hard as they could, winter was on them before they were ready. Cold winds blew through cracks in the cabin and food grew scarce. The family managed to make it through the winter by eating food brought by neighbors, and the deer, turkeys, and other wild game Owen killed.

In the spring he cleared a small plot of land and planted corn, but squirrels and birds ate most of it and an early frost killed the rest. The second winter was almost as harsh as the first.

"We had some hardships to undergo," the uncomplaining Owen said later, "but they appear greater in history than they were in reality."

At last, life began to improve. Owen was hired as a surveyor and made frequent trips into the forest to mark out land around Hudson. He sometimes trav-

John Brown's father, Owen Brown.

eled sixty or seventy miles and was gone for two weeks at a time.

With his father absent so much and his mother busy with the unending chores of a frontier wife and mother, young John was often left on his own.

He eagerly took advantage of his freedom "to be quite a rambler in the wild new country finding birds and Squirels, & sometimes a wild Turkeys nest."

Though many whites hated Native Americans as much as they hated black people, John took after his father, who found them "very friendly and I beleave [they were] a benifet rather than injery there [were] some Persons that seemed disposed to quarel with the Indians but I never had, they brought us Venson Turkeys Fish and the like sometimes wanted bread or meal more than they could pay for, but were faithful to pay their debts . . ."

Once Owen helped swear out a warrant for murder against whites who pursued and attacked a group of Native Americans, killing one and injuring several others. His action was unpopular with some settlers, but he refused to back down.

At first, John was afraid of the Native Americans he met in the forest, but he soon found them so friendly he sought them out, learned "a trifle" of their language, and spent as much time with them as possible. They were the lonely child's first friends, and he never forgot them.

Near the end of his life, writing of himself in the third person, John Brown still remembered when "a poor *Indian boy* gave him a Yellow Marble the first he had ever seen. This he thought a great deal of; & kept it a good while; but at last *he lost it* beyond recovery. *It took years to heal the wound*; & I think he cried at times about it."

John was an awkward, solitary child who was especially close to his mother. She died shortly after giving birth to a daughter who lived just a few hours, and he felt devastated. He was just eight years old at the time.

Her death, he said later, was "complete & permanent for not withstanding his Father again married to a sensible, intelligent, & on many accounts a very estimable woman: *yet he never adopted her in feeling*: but continued to pine after his own Mother for years."

It was the way he would react to many events in his life: feeling their emotional reverberations to the depths of his soul, but sharing those emotions with few others. In this, he was like his father.

Few outside the family knew the depth of Owen Brown's grief over the loss of his wife but, more than forty years later, he said of that day: "This sean all most makes my heart blead now."

Owen went quietly about the business of surveying land for new settlers and resolving quarrels over boundaries. This soon allowed him to save enough money to build a better house and a tannery, where he taught young John how to make leather out of the hides of deer, wolves, dogs, and other animals. Left with six children to raise, Owen married twenty-year-old Sally Root the next year.

In the months that followed the death of his mother, John's increasing anger and aggressiveness were shown in many ways.

A classmate remembered how the boys in Hudson formed rival gangs based on the political beliefs of their fathers. The "little Federalists" were composed of John and others whose fathers opposed slavery, while the "little Democrats" were composed of boys whose fathers supported the Virginia slaveholders, Jefferson, and Madison. The two groups attended separate log schools.

One day the little Democrats began pelting John and his future brother-in-law, Milton Lusk, with wet snowballs.

They "were hard and hurt 'masterly,'" remembered Lusk. "John stood this for a while — then he rushed alone upon the little Democrats, and drove them all before him into their schoolhouse. He did not seem angry, but there was such force and mastery in what he did, that everything gave way before him."

John's bitterness and anger lasted almost two years, when it began to be alleviated by something he would cherish for the rest of his life: reading.

An older friend offered him the use of his small library, Brown said later, again referring to himself in the third person, "by which he acquired some taste for reading: which formed the principle part of his early education: & diverted him in great measure from bad company. . . ."

The reading helped him gain confidence, because his newfound search for knowledge led him to seek the company of older people, who treated him in a "kind manner . . . at their houses; & in conversation; which was a great relief on account of his extreme bashfulness."

But the shyness, especially around women, would always be part of him.

He spent little time in school, preferring hard work and helping his father. When the War of 1812 broke out with England, Owen Brown became a beef contractor for the American forces in Detroit. Although John was only twelve, he rounded up wild steers and other cattle in the wilderness and helped his father drive them to army outposts in Michigan Territory.

John was pleased at being treated like an adult and was thrilled at being able to hang around the soldiers and listen to them talk of war. But soon their profanity and lack of discipline revolted him. He was so disgusted by their conduct that when he was old enough to take part in his community's required militia drills, he paid fines, like the nonviolent Quakers, rather than participate.

And on one journey he took by himself, he saw the evil of slavery his father had always talked about.

John said he stayed "for a short time with a very gentlemanly landlord" who later became a United States marshal. The man owned a slave boy about the same age as John.

But while the man "made a great pet of John: brought him to table with his . . . friends; called their attention to every little smart thing he *said or did*; & to the fact of his being more than a hundred miles from home with a company of cattle alone," the slave owner's reaction to the black boy he owned was entirely different.

As the demand for cotton increased, so did the value of slaves.

John said the boy, who was very intelligent and did "numerous little acts of kindness" for him, "was badly clothed, poorly fed," and routinely beaten by the owner "with Iron Shovels or any other thing that came first to hand."

John was haunted by the boy's mistreatment, and "the wretched, hopeless condition, of *Fatherless & Motherless* slave *children*: for such children have neither Fathers or Mothers to protect, & provide for them. . . . *is God their Father?*"

The experience seared the reality of slavery into

his mind and emotions in a way he would never forget.

The next few years saw John work hard and grow into a tall, lean teenager who often supervised the workers in his father's tannery. The employees were all much older, but they readily followed his orders.

In 1816, he enrolled in a school in Plainfield, Massachusetts, to try to prepare for college and eventually study for the ministry. Owen Brown had lost most of his money after the War of 1812, but he gave his son a horse for the journey and told him to sell it for tuition and board once he reached Plainfield.

John arrived at the school carrying "a piece of sole leather about a foot square, which he had himself tanned for seven years, to resole his boots."

He studied hard and transferred to Morris Academy in Litchfield, Connecticut, after a few months. There he spent hours each night trying to learn the Latin and Greek he had ignored while a schoolboy in Hudson.

But the long hours of reading by candelight hurt his vision and he developed a severe inflammation of the eyes. This, combined with the lack of money and the poor quality of his previous education, forced him to give up his dream and return to Hudson.

If he felt disappointment, he apparently kept it to himself. But a friend said the disappointment was there because "with him it was one of his *principles,* never to yield a point, or abandon anything he had fixed his purpose upon."

Even forty years later, writing about his youth, he never said a word about either Plainfield or Morris Academy.

John went back to working for his father at the tannery and on the farm. He especially liked tending the sheep and talking about the fine cattle he would one day own.

In 1818, he and Levi Blakeslee moved out of Owen's house, and built their own cabin and tannery. John loved to cook and prepared all their meals. It was common practice for employees to live with their employers, and as the tannery prospered several men came to live with John and Levi. He enlarged the cabin and hired a Mrs. Lusk and her daughter, Dianthe, to do the cooking and housework.

Dianthe was one year younger than John, and just as religious. Every day she went alone to a special place in the woods to pray. She was also, he said admiringly, a "remarkably plain but neat, industrious and economical girl, of excellent character and remarkable piety."

They were married in 1820 in the Congregational Church in Hudson. John, Jr., the first of his and Dianthe's seven children, was born in 1821, and was followed in 1823 by Jason, and in 1824 by Owen.

"The first thing I can remember is being rocked to sleep in my father's arms to his singing of 'Blow Ye the Trumpet Blow!' John, Jr., said. "... For thirty years there was a baby in the house, and he sang us all to sleep ... with that same hymn:

"Blow ye the trumpet, blow
The gladly solemn sound;
Let all the nations know
To earth's remotest bound,
The year of Jubilee is come,
Return, ye ransomed sinners, home!"

Brown taught Sunday school, made church attendance compulsory for his workers, and required them to worship in the cabin every morning. His religious convictions also led him to believe, said one of his workers, that it was "as much his duty to help a Negro make his escape as it was to help catch a horse thief."

There were few fugitive slaves in Ohio at this time, but their numbers were beginning to grow. During the early part of John Brown's life, it seemed that slavery was dying out on its own because it was no longer profitable. Most slaves grew tobacco, rice, and indigo, and there was only a limited market for such crops.

By 1805, every Northern state had either abolished slavery or made plans for its gradual abolition. And although slavery remained a powerful institution in the South, manumission of slaves (releasing them from slavery) became more widespread as slavery grew less profitable. In addition, many slaves were allowed to buy their freedom.

All of that changed with the coming of the Industrial Revolution. New machinery created a huge textile industry in England and New England, and the industry in turn created an enormous market for cotton.

It was difficult for slave owners to make money raising the crop, however. It took a slave an entire day to clean the sticky seeds from a few pounds of cotton, but the invention of the cotton gin (short for

A 1793 drawing of Whitney's cotton gin.

"engine") meant one slave could clean hundreds of pounds a day. The result was an economic and political revolution that made cotton the most important crop in the South, and slavery the most important issue in American life.

The price of slaves quickly doubled in what soon came to be called the Cotton Kingdom. Cotton was the mainstay of the South's economy, and formed a vital part of the business of financial centers in New York, manufacturing in New England, and the increasing trade with the rapidly developing states and territories in the West.

Slaves, who had previously clung to the hope that they or their children might one day be free, now knew they were too valuable to ever be free.

Cotton was best grown on large plantations, and there the slaves were treated more harshly than ever. During harvest season, said one slave, the crack of the lash and the cries of men and women could be heard from sunup to sundown.

In the impersonal atmosphere of these large plantations, black families also faced the increased threat of members being sold to different masters, as slave owners constantly looked for stronger, more productive slaves for the backbreaking labor. Children were often sold so slave owners wouldn't have to feed and house them before they became fully productive adults.

"My brothers and sisters were bid off first, and one

by one, while my mother, paralyzed by grief, held me by the hand," said one man who was sold from his mother when he was five years old. "Her turn came, and she was bought by Isaac Riley . . . Then I was offered to the assembled purchasers. My mother . . . pushed through the crowd, while the bidding for me was going on . . . She fell at his feet . . . entreating him . . . (to) spare to her one, at least, of her little ones. Will it, can it be believed that this man . . . was capable of . . . disengaging himself from her with such violent blows and kicks, as to reduce her to the necessity of creeping out of his reach, and mingling the groan of bodily suffering with the sob of a breaking heart?"

Remembering this scene years later, the man declared: "I seem to see and hear my poor weeping mother now."

And so, as slavery was strengthened, more and more fugitives risked their lives to escape to the North, but even there they weren't safe.

The Fugitive Slave Law, passed while George Washington was president, had made it a crime to harbor escaping slaves or prevent their arrest. But many whites and free blacks helped them anyway, providing food, shelter, and directions to the next safe house on what came to be called the Underground Railroad.

Escaping slaves who made their way to John Brown's house were always welcome. John, Jr., remembered the first black people he ever saw: a man and his wife who knocked on the door one night when he was four or five years old.

"Mother gave the poor creatures some supper," he said, "but they thought themselves pursued, and were uneasy. Presently father heard the trampling of horses crossing a bridge on one of the main roads, half a mile off; so he took his guests out the back door and down into the swamp near the brook, to hide, giving them arms to defend themselves, but returning to the house to await the event."

The horsemen turned out to be neighbors going into town, but when Brown tried to find the couple in the dark, he was unsuccessful until "finally he was guided to the spot by the sound of the man's heart throbbing for fear of capture."

Such visitors were rare, but would become more frequent in the years ahead. Most of John Brown's time continued to be taken up with business and religious activities. He bought several acres of farmland near the tannery, tore down his cabin, and built a large house with a garden and orchard.

Dianthe began to suffer physically and emotionally from the hard work of caring for her family and the employees. Depending on the number of workers at the tannery, she often had to cook for as many as fifteen people.

As her health grew worse, Brown did much of the

cooking and housework, and often watched over her at night with a gentleness his children remembered decades later.

In 1826, he moved his family to Randolph Township in the Pennsylvania wilderness, just a few miles from the Western Reserve. The land was so wild, said one neighbor, that bears roamed the woods and you could hear "the long howl of the wolf as he prowled about the sheepfolds and the barns in the darkness of the night."

Within four months, Brown had cleared twenty-five acres of woods, built a tannery with eighteen vats, a two-room log house, and a large barn with a secret room in it for hiding fugitive slaves. The room was so cleverly concealed, a person could stand on top of it and not even know the hiding place was there.

Antislavery societies were being formed in many states, and they held a national meeting in 1826. Most called for the gradual abolition of slavery, but for few, if any, legal and political rights for black people. Members of a society in southern Ohio stood alone in urging the immediate end of slavery and full citizenship for black Americans.

John Brown took no part in the societies or their meetings, preferring — as he always would — to keep his fight against slavery under his control.

Far to the south on a Maryland plantation, a six-year-old black boy named Frederick Bailey Washington wept and pondered over the cruelty of slavery when he "saw the slave-driver whip a slave woman, cut the blood out of her neck, and heard her piteous cries . . ."

One day the paths of the boy and John Brown would cross, but that day was still far off. For now the youth, knowing the danger of speaking out, kept his thoughts of freedom to himself.

Over three hundred miles to the north, John Brown was becoming known to his Randolph neighbors as a man who asked each newcomer "whether he was an observer of the Sabbath, opposed to Slavery and a Supporter of the Gospel and common Schools, if So all was right with him, if not he was looked upon by Brown with Suspicion."

But, like Frederick Washington, John Brown also kept many of his thoughts about slavery and freedom to himself.

CHAPTER TWO

◼

I CONSECRATE MY LIFE

During the next few years, Brown surveyed new roads, built a school and paid the teacher's salary, helped organize a church, became the first person in the county to raise purebred sheep and cattle, and built a thriving tannery business.

He also helped establish a post office at Randolph (now New Richmond), and was appointed its first postmaster by President John Quincy Adams. Brown soon gained a reputation for honesty and for the high quality of his leather, which he refused to sell if he thought it contained any water.

This time in Randolph would be the happiest and most prosperous years of his life, and his steadily growing family was at the center of his happiness. In the evenings, he loved to hold the children on his knees, and sing to them.

But even in these years of happiness, there was also much sorrow. Dianthe gave birth to seven children, but only five lived to adulthood. One died in 1831 at the age of four and the last, a boy, died a few hours after being born in August, 1832. This was the harsh reality for women of that time: long hours of toil in home and farm that aged them prematurely, high infant mortality rates, and death during childbirth.

In the hours after Dianthe gave birth to their last child, John Brown watched helplessly as her life slipped away.

"Last night about eleven o'clock my affectionate, dutiful and faithful Dianthe bade 'farewell to Earth,'" he wrote his father. "At her request the children were brought to her and she with heavenly composure gave faithful advice to each. . . . Tomorrow she is to lay beside our little son."

Brown buried Dianthe and their last child in the family graveyard on the highest part of the land.

In the months that followed he felt "more & more unfit for everything," including taking care of the children. Sometimes he did not leave the house for days, silently "growing numb" to everyone and everything around him.

He didn't care if the tannery failed or not, and felt "verry little" emotion when a friend took the children to live with him and his new bride. But slowly Brown's love for life began to return.

He moved his children back into the house and

hired a housekeeper who brought along her sister, a large, quiet sixteen-year-old named Mary Ann Day.

Brown gradually became attracted to her and, though he was twice her age, handed her a letter one day containing a marriage proposal. She was unde- cided at first, perhaps frightened by his stern de- meanor, but she finally said yes.

Mary Ann Brown (wife of John Brown), with their two daughters, Annie (left) and Sarah (right).

They were married in June, 1833, and would remain married for the rest of Brown's life. The next year, Mary gave birth to the first of their thirteen children, a daughter named Sarah.

Once more he began to pour his energies into business and community activities, and into enjoying his family. And although he was as opposed as ever to slavery, he remained curiously aloof from the increasingly divisive struggle to end it.

In 1831, that struggle had been changed forever by two events: the revolt of Nat Turner and the publication of the first issue of William Lloyd Garrison's antislavery weekly, *The Liberator*.

Two years earlier, whites throughout the country and especially in the South had been stunned by a seventy-six-page book written by a black man named David Walker. *David Walker's Appeal* called on slaves to violently overthrow slavery, declaring "it is no more harm for you to kill a man, who is trying to kill you, than it is for you to take a drink of water when thirsty. . . ."

White Southerners were so alarmed by the *Appeal*, they convened secret legislative sessions to pass laws against it. Georgia made it a crime punishable by death to introduce or circulate literature calling on slaves to fight for their freedom. Virginia barred black ministers from preaching because some were suspected of reading the *Appeal* to their congregations.

Whites in the North were also dismayed at the

thought of blacks seizing their freedom by violence. The *Appeal* was condemned by white abolitionists, including Garrison, who believed that slavery could be ended by "pricking the slaveholders' conscience" until they repented of the sin of slavery.

But even though Garrison advocated nonviolence to end slavery, proslavery forces were appalled at his attack on the "conspiracy of silence" that had always protected their social, economic, and political power.

If Garrison's words appalled them, however, Nat Turner's actions terrified them.

Less than seven months after *The Liberator* began publication in Boston, Turner led his band of black freedom fighters in an uprising in the county of Southampton, Virginia. They killed almost all the whites they came across, sparing only a poor family that owned no slaves. By the time Turner and his men were finished, at least fifty-seven whites lay dead.

State forces were joined by United States soldiers, sailors, and marines in putting down the rebellion, which lasted forty hours. President Andrew Jackson, a slave owner, dispatched three United States warships to help the Virginia slave owners.

Enraged troops and civilians swept through the countryside, indiscriminately torturing and slaughtering black people. They branded some with hot irons, mutilated the faces of others, smashed bones, cut off heads and stuck them on posts. Nat Turner's wife was tortured and beaten.

During the next several months, slaves throughout the South were arrested, beaten, and killed by owners who feared the slaves were thinking of rebelling.

The message to slaves was that any attempt to fight for freedom would be met with the most savage force imaginable, including the entire military might of the United States government.

The rebellion so terrified whites in Virginia and throughout the South, that legislatures secretly debated ending slavery.

Instead of ending slavery, the slave owners in Virginia and throughout the South made it harsher than

Nat Turner led a slave revolt in Southampton County, Virginia.

ever. From the time of Turner's revolt until the Civil War, manumission virtually stopped, laws governing the slaves' lives were enforced more stringently than ever, and it was made a crime for slaves to learn to read and write (though thousands did in secret schools in the middle of the night), or for white people to teach them.

A white woman in Norfolk, Virginia, named Margaret Douglass was found guilty of "one of the vilest crimes that ever disgraced a society," according to the court. Her crime was teaching Kate, "a slave girl, to read the Bible. No enlightened society can exist where such offenses go unpunished."

Antiblack riots swept through many cities, including Boston and Philadelphia, where white mobs destroyed the homes of black people, burned a church and meetinghouse, and beat any black person they could find.

"Press, church, magistrates, clergymen and devils are against us," wrote a black man in Philadelphia to a white abolitionist friend. "The measure of our suffering is full. . . . Despair, black as the pall of death, hangs over us, and the bloody *will* is in the heart of the community to destroy us."

The argument over slavery raged in cities, towns, and villages throughout the North, but John Brown at times seemed almost unaware of it as he went about his daily chores.

Elizur Wright, a former schoolmate of John Brown and a professor at Western Reserve College, took over as secretary of the American Anti-Slavery Society. Other antislavery men Brown's age were distributing abolitionist literature, speaking out in their communities, and helping organize meetings.

But though anger over the fate of slavery swirled all around him and even involved his father (who resigned from the board of Western Reserve College and helped found Oberlin College in a dispute over slavery), John Brown's world continued to revolve around his business endeavors and his family.

But despite his silence, his feelings about racial injustice were as strong as ever, as some of his neighbors discovered one day.

Native Americans from New York State used to spend their winters camping near town, so they could hunt in the vast woods. Brown often gave them food and hay, which angered some of the people in Randolph. One day, several of the settlers showed up at his house with guns, and asked him to help drive away the Native Americans.

"I will have nothing to do with so mean an act," an outraged Brown replied. "I would sooner take my gun and help drive *you* out of the country."

His son, Jason, said it was the first time he'd ever seen his father really angry.

And although Brown said little publicly about

slavery, he had obviously thought a lot about it. His ideas for fighting it were as nonviolent as Garrison's, and revolved around education.

In a letter to his brother Frederick, written in 1834, Brown said he had been trying "to devise some means whereby I might do something in a practical way for my poor fellow-men who are in bondage. . . ."

Mary and his sons had agreed with him to either adopt a black boy "and bring him up as we do our own . . . give him a good . . . education," or try to find some way "to get a school a–going here for blacks . . ."

Although Brown didn't mention it, he was aware that such schools could be dangerous to operate. Several months before, a young Quaker woman named Prudence Crandall admitted a black girl into her Female Seminary in Canterbury, Connecticut.

When white parents responded by threatening to withdraw their daughters, she followed William Lloyd Garrison's suggestion that she close the seminary and reopen it as a school for black girls.

Residents tossed manure into the school well, refused to allow the girls to attend the local church, fired pistols near them, threatened them with whipping for allegedly violating a little-used vagrancy law, and cursed them whenever they stepped outside.

Prudence Crandall was tried and jailed for violating a hurriedly passed state law making it illegal to teach out-of-state black students. (Her sentence was later overturned on a technicality.)

William Lloyd Garrison published the famous antislavery weekly, The Liberator.

Finally, a mob armed with clubs and iron bars assaulted the school while the girls slept, smashing ninety panes of glass. The attack left Miss Crandall and the students "terror-stricken," and she was forced to close the school.

In proposing his school for black children, John Brown was very aware of the need for community support.

"Write me how you would like to join me," he told Frederick, "and try to get . . . some first-rate abolitionist families with you."

A few months later, Brown found himself without

enough money to operate his tannery, let alone start a school. Money became so tight throughout the area that he was unable to sell anything for cash, collect debts owed him, or pay his bills.

A wealthy businessman in Franklin Mills (now Kent), Ohio, invited him to form a partnership in the tanning industry, and Brown moved his family back to Ohio. The partnership failed to work out, however.

His return to Ohio coincided with an almost frenzied growth in the nation's economy. Factories were springing up throughout the North to make shoes, clothes, and other items people formerly made for themselves. The almost four-hundred-mile-long Erie Canal, completed in 1825, linked the Midwest with New York City and the Atlantic Coast. It allowed midwestern farmers to sell their produce to people hundreds of miles away, whereas previously they could only sell to nearby customers.

Other canals were being planned or built in Pennsylvania and Ohio, and speculators staked out land along their proposed routes, for towns and factories. John Brown was soon caught up in this speculation fever, buying farms and dividing them into lots he hoped to sell for large profits.

He had no money, and his purchases, like those of the majority of speculators throughout the country, were made by signing promissory notes to a local bank.

Years later he said of his actions, "The practical effect of this false doctrine" (borrowing instead of "*pay as you go*") "has been to keep me like a toad under a harrow most of my business life. . . ."

His dreams of prosperity came crashing down in 1837, when a depression hit the country and over six hundred banks failed. John Brown, like countless others, was broke and would remain in debt the rest of his life.

He was now thirty-seven, with a wife and nine children to care for. He floundered around for the next several years, trying to feed his family by doing everything from raising racehorses (which he gave up because his conscience bothered him) to buying cattle and driving them to markets in the East.

During this time, although he said little publicly about slavery and racism, his feelings sometimes burst to the surface.

He hired a black man and woman to work for him, and one Sunday when the woman went to church, she was told to sit in the back.

"This aroused father's indignation at once," his daughter Ruth said. "He asked both of them to go the next Sunday; they followed the family in, and he seated them in his pew. The whole congregation were shocked; the minister looked angry; but I remember father's firm, determined look. . . ."

Around this same time, an incident occurred that shocked John Brown and much of the nation. A

young white minister from Maine, named Elijah
Lovejoy, settled in St. Louis, in the slave state of Missouri, and began editing a Presbyterian weekly newspaper called the *Observer*. St. Louis, like many cities
both North and South, depended on trade with slave
owners for much of its economic life.

In the paper, Lovejoy denounced slavery as both a
cruel form of oppression and a sin against God. Angry residents wrecked his office after he wrote an article protesting the burning to death of a black man
by a mob. Lovejoy was forced to flee the city with his
wife, Celia, and their baby son, after the mob invaded and smashed their home.

He moved his family to Alton in the free state of
Illinois, but he and his home were again attacked and
his new printing press destroyed. He bought a third
press, and an angry mob broke into his office, scattered the type, and threw the printing press into the
Mississippi River.

But Lovejoy refused to be intimidated and, with
the financial help of abolitionists throughout the
North, bought a fourth printing press.

"The cry of the oppressed has entered, not only
into my ears, but into my soul so that while I live I
cannot hold my peace," he wrote his mother.

One night while he was away on an errand, a mob
marched on his home. He heard their howling as he
returned, then saw them smashing his windows. He
raced past the cursing men and into the house, des-

perately shouting his wife's name as he ran from room to room. Finally he found her, terrified and huddled face down in the middle of the attic, trying to shield their son with her body.

A few days later, a mob encouraged by the town's business and political leaders killed Lovejoy and threw his fourth printing press into the river.

Twenty-eight-year-old Abraham Lincoln, who had recently started practicing law in Illinois, said that Lovejoy's murder was "the most important single event that ever happened in the new world."

Ex-president John Quincy Adams, now a staunch antislavery congressman from Massachusetts, said Lovejoy's murder sent "a shock as of an earthquake throughout this continent."

Many white Americans who cared little about slavery or the power slaveholders exercised over the lives of black people were outraged and horrified to learn that slaveholders could exercise that same power over them.

"A few white victims must be sacrificed to open the eyes of the nation, and to show the tyranny of our laws," William Lloyd Garrison had predicted years before, and now his prediction was coming true.

Meetings were held throughout the North to protest Lovejoy's murder, and John Brown and his father were among those who packed the Congregational Church in Hudson.

John Brown sat silently in the back of the church

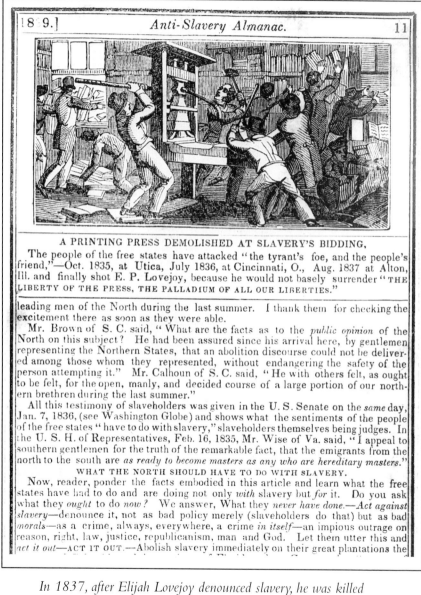

A PRINTING PRESS DEMOLISHED AT SLAVERY'S BIDDING,

The people of the free states have attacked "the tyrant's foe, and the people's friend,"—Oct. 1835, at Utica, July 1836, at Cincinnati, O., Aug. 1837 at Alton, Ill. and finally shot E. P. Lovejoy, because he would not basely surrender "THE LIBERTY OF THE PRESS, THE PALLADIUM OF ALL OUR LIBERTIES."

leading men of the North during the last summer. I thank them for checking the excitement there as soon as they were able.

Mr. Brown of S. C. said, "What are the facts as to the *public opinion* of the North on this subject? He had been assured since his arrival here, by gentlemen representing the Northern States, that an abolition discourse could not be delivered among those whom they represented, without endangering the safety of the person attempting it." Mr. Calhoun of S. C. said, "He with others felt, as ought to be felt, for the open, manly, and decided course of a large portion of our northern brethren during the last summer."

All this testimony of slaveholders was given in the U. S. Senate on the *same* day, Jan. 7, 1836, (see Washington Globe) and shows what the sentiments of the people of the free states "have to do with slavery," slaveholders themselves being judges. In the U. S. H. of Representatives, Feb. 16, 1835, Mr. Wise of Va. said, "I appeal to southern gentlemen for the truth of the remarkable fact, that the emigrants from the north to the south are *as ready to become masters as any who are hereditary masters.*"

WHAT THE NORTH SHOULD HAVE TO DO WITH SLAVERY.

Now, reader, ponder the facts embodied in this article and learn what the free states have had to do and are doing not only *with* slavery but *for* it. Do you ask what they *ought* to do *now?* We answer, What they *never have done.—Act against slavery*—denounce it, not as bad policy merely (slaveholders do that) but as bad *morals*—as a crime, always, everywhere, a crime *in itself*—an impious outrage on reason, right, law, justice, republicanism, man and God. Let them utter this and *act it out*—ACT IT OUT.—Abolish slavery immediately on their great plantations the

In 1837, after Elijah Lovejoy denounced slavery, he was killed and his printing press was destroyed.

throughout the afternoon as speaker after speaker, including his father, denounced slavery and spoke of Lovejoy's courage. Suddenly, just as Owen Brown was about to end the meeting with a prayer, Brown stood up and raised his right hand as if taking an oath.

"Here before God," he said slowly, "in the presence of these witnesses, I consecrate my life to the destruction of slavery."

Then he sat down and his father, tears flowing down his cheeks, closed the meeting with "a great prayer" for Lovejoy and for freedom.

John Brown continued to dream of freedom for all slaves in the years to come, while a young black farmer named Dangerfield Newby dreamed of freedom for his wife, Harriet, and their children.

Though Newby was free, his wife and children were held in slavery. He worked every job he could find, trying to save enough money to buy their freedom, but he could never save enough.

"Oh, Dear Dangerfield," she would write him one day far in the future, "com this fall without fail, *monny* or no *monney*. I want to see you so much. That is one bright hope I have before me. . . ."

It would take over two decades, but the vow Brown made that afternoon in a church in Hudson would finally lead him to both Newby and the town near where Harriet and Newby's children lived: Harpers Ferry, Virginia.

CHAPTER THREE

THE BASIS OF MY PLAN

The debate over slavery now raged throughout the country, sparking antiabolition riots that were often supported by Northern businessmen whose profits depended on slavery.

The argument was also fueled by Congressional refusal to allow antislavery petitions to be debated in Congress, and by the attempt to have Texas brought into the Union as a slaveholding state.

"It is . . . to be considered that at this time the most dangerous of all the subjects for public contention is the slavery question," John Quincy Adams wrote in his diary.

John Brown was acutely aware of the debate swirling all around him, often discussing the issues with his family, but once again he focused his energy on financial survival.

Almost all of his property had been taken, and

now he tried desperately to earn or borrow enough money to hold onto what remained. Twice he left home for months at a time, driving cattle six hundred miles to Connecticut, and traveling to New York City and Boston to meet with bankers.

For the first time he walked streets where proslavery mobs had roamed, such as the one that dragged Garrison through the streets of Boston in 1835 with a rope around his neck, and burned down Pennsylvania Hall in Philadelphia just a few months before Brown came east.

Three days after the hall was dedicated by aboli-

Pennsylvania Hall in Philadelphia was burned by proslavery mobs.

tionists, a mob, led by white Southern students study-ing medicine in Philadelphia, ransacked and burned the building.

Poet John Greenleaf Whittier, a Quaker and abo-litionist editor whose offices were in the hall, fled for his life. Then he disguised himself with a white wig and returned to rescue his papers. A few hours later, as dawn finally ended the long, terrifying night, Whittier wrote:

"The beautiful temple consecrated to Liberty has been offered a smoking sacrifice to the Demon of Slavery. . . . Let the abhorred deed speak for itself. Let all men see by what frail tenure they hold prop-erty and life in a land overshadowed by the curse of slavery. . . ."

The Wall Street area John Brown stalked in pursuit of money was routinely stalked by those in pursuit of human beings: slave catchers hunting black men, women, and children who had escaped from slavery.

A few weeks before Brown's arrival in New York City in December, 1838, twenty-one-year-old Fred-erick Bailey Washington (now calling himself Freder-ick Bailey) reached the city after finally accomplishing his long-planned escape.

"My chains were broken, and the victory brought me unspeakable joy," he remembered. "But my glad-ness was short-lived, for I was not yet out of the reach and power of the slaveholders."

He met a black man he'd known in slavery, and learned that danger lurked on every street.

The man told him "there were hired men ever on the lookout for fugitives; that I must trust no man with my secret; that I must not think of going either upon the wharves, or into any colored boarding house, for all such places were closely watched. . . ."

Bailey was finally befriended by a stranger who took him to the home of a black man named David Ruggles, director of the New York Committee of Vigilance and one of the Underground Railroad's leading "conductors."

Ruggles had helped hundreds of slaves escape and was so hated by slave owners that they once broke down his door and tried to kidnap him, but he escaped by crawling through a window.

Ruggles arranged transportation for Frederick Bailey to New Bedford, Massachusetts, where he soon changed his name to Frederick Douglass, labored at any job he could find, and began attending antislavery lectures.

The month Douglass arrived in New Bedford, John Brown was less than sixty miles north in Boston, still trying unsuccessfully to secure a loan. He returned home the next month, then drove another herd of cattle back east a few weeks later.

He missed his family terribly, as he would every time he left them in the years to come.

"Say to my little folks I want very much to see them," he wrote Mary, "and tell Ruth and Fred not to forget the [Bible] verse their father taught them last."

In another letter he wrote: "My unceaseing and anxious care for the present and everlasting welfare of evry [member] of my family seems to be threefold as I get separated farther and farther from them."

He was also afraid of his family's reaction if he failed to secure the loan and they became "very poor; for our debts must be paid, if paid at a sacrifice. . . ."

"I have left no stone unturned to place my affairs in a more settled and comfortable shape," he wrote shortly before starting home, "and now should I, after all my sacrifice of body and mind be compelled to return, a very poor man, how would my family receive me?"

In the summer of 1839 he returned to Ohio and was, as he had feared, a very poor man. Even worse, he had taken money advanced to him to buy wool for the New England Woolen Company, and used it to pay his debts.

At first some of his partners considered prosecuting him for theft, but finally decided Brown was an honest man who had made a foolish mistake. One partner told him that someone as ardently antislavery as he was could not engage in any wrongdoing without harming the cause.

Brown agreed and said, "I feel grateful to learn

that you have feelings of tenderness towards one that has abused . . . your confidence, injured your business and what is worse than all wounded a holy and great suffering cause. . . ."

Even in the midst of all this trouble, however, Brown found happiness in finally fulfilling a lifelong dream: to become a shepherd.

In his travels in New England, he somehow managed to buy several pure-blooded Saxony sheep he hoped would become the basis of a great flock.

"He often spoke of the life of the shepherd being favorable to religious meditation," John, Jr., said.

Brown loved the details of caring for sheep: curing them of illness, washing them for hours at a time to remove dirt from the wool, then shearing them in specially enclosed spaces so the wool wouldn't get contaminated.

In his long nights of solitude as a shepherd, John Brown continued to think about his "greatest and principal object" — the abolition of slavery.

One night he told his family he intended to make war on slavery, though he didn't know how or when. But "when the 'call' came," John, Jr., remembered him saying, "his wife was to consider herself a widow, his children committed to the care of Him who fed the ravens.

"And then he *knelt* in prayer to ask a blessing on his resolution. I say *knelt*, for I never saw him kneel again, either before or after that time."

John Brown's son, John Jr.

Mary joined the three oldest boys, John, Jr., Jason, and Owen, in agreeing to devote their lives to ending slavery.

"As the other children grew older the matter was explained to them, and not one failed him," John, Jr., said. "As we married, our wives and husbands were converted. There was a Brown family conspiracy that existed unsuspected for twenty-one years to break the power of slavery."

Brown had decided he would never again engage in a business he couldn't leave on two weeks notice to pursue his goal. In the meantime, he would try to make as much money as possible to provide for his family after he was gone.

The next few years saw a continuation of his financial struggles. At one point he journeyed to Virginia to survey a huge tract of land owned by Oberlin College, with the idea of eventually settling his family there. Nothing came of the plan, but he saw Virginia for the first time as he walked the Appalachian foothills two hundred miles west of Harpers Ferry.

"I like the country as well as I expected," he wrote Mary and the children, "and its inhabitants rather better. . . ."

In the years to come he returned to Virginia several times on business, and was increasingly impressed with the natural fortifications the mountains could afford a small band of armed, determined men.

He finally filed for bankruptcy, which a court granted in 1842, leaving him with nothing but a few household objects, some food for the winter, several Bibles, and nineteen sheep. Though he was under no legal obligation, he promised to pay his creditors as soon as he was able.

Battered and sometimes feeling almost broken by his unrelenting financial problems, Brown turned to his family for solace. He now had twelve children, ranging in age from twenty-two-year-old John, Jr., to one-year-old Austin.

He often put the younger ones on his knees and sang hymns to them, or asked the older children to read him a Psalm. When his "affectionate aged, & honored Father" stayed overnight, Brown tucked him into bed, and then got up during the night to make sure he was warm. If any of the children were sick, he stayed up all night nursing them.

"A man can hardly get into difficulties too big to be surmounted if he has a firm foothold at home," he taught his children. "Remember that. . . ."

Through all his troubles, his wife was so supportive Brown told her "you are *really* my better half."

Mary was as religious as he was, reading her Bible every day and trusting that God would give her strength to bear whatever happened. Both soon needed all the strength they could find, for suddenly in September, 1843, four of their children died of dysentery in less than three weeks.

Six-year-old Charles, described by his brother Salmon as "quiet as a cat, but brave as a tiger," died on the 4th. He was followed by the baby, Austin, on the 21st; three-year-old Peter on the 22nd; and nine-year-old Sarah, Mary's first-born, on the 23rd.

"That was the time in my life when all my religion, all my philosophy, and all my faith in God's goodness were put to the test," Mary recalled almost forty years later. "Yet even in these trials God upheld me."

Brown buried the children side by side not far from the house and then wrote John, Jr., who was away at school, "God has seen fit to visit us with the pestilence since you left us, and Four of our number sleep in the dust. . . . This has been to us all a bitter cup indeed, and we have drunk deeply, but still the Lord reigneth and blessed be his great and holy name forever."

He was now forty-three, and a man with "a fearless, challenging look, a firm mouth, a jaw thrust forward. No one could see him and not know him a resolute man," said John, Jr.

He was more determined than ever to make money, not only to provide for his family, but to finance his plan to end slavery. In 1844, he formed a partnership in the wool business with Simon Perkins, Jr., of Akron, and the Brown-Perkins flock soon won a reputation as "the finest and most perfect flock of Saxon sheep in the United States."

Brown traveled throughout the Ohio Valley, including into northwestern Virginia, to buy sheep, but he also used these trips to help slaves escape.

"I've seen him come in at night with [a] gang of five or six blacks that he had piloted all the way from the [Ohio] river, . . ." said a neighbor. "He would appear on the streets without saying a word to anyone about it. But let any slaveholder discover the whereabouts of his charges and attempt to take them back, and he would fight like a lion."

During his travels he talked to hundreds of farmers, who complained that Eastern manufacturers were paying too little for their wool. Brown suggested they form a cooperative to give them more bargaining power and, at their suggestion, he agreed to run such an enterprise.

Perkins supplied the capital, and in 1846 the firm of Perkins & Brown opened an office and warehouse in Springfield, Massachusetts. Brown, acting as an agent for the farmers who sent him their wool, tried to force higher prices from the manufacturers.

Most of the family stayed in Ohio, but Jason came to help and was soon followed by John, Jr.

"He had a big brick warehouse," John, Jr., said, "was the most important middleman in the business, but the family lived in an old frame house in a mean street, and as poorly as laborers. Not an unnecessary penny was spent, except for education."

Brown worked at least twelve hours every day, except Sundays, and wrote Mary whenever he could. His letters were filled with longing for his wife and children, and with guilt for being absent from them.

Sometimes Mary cut sentences from the letters that told of his affection for her, and carefully put them away among her keepsakes.

"I do not forget the firm attachment of her who has remained my fast, and faithful affectionate friend," he wrote. "When I reflect on these things together with the verry considerable difference in our age, as well as all the follies, and faults with which I am justly chargeable, I really admire your constancy."

In November, 1846, he returned from a business

trip to find a letter telling him his baby daughter, Amelia, had been accidentally scalded to death by Ruth.

The news left Brown "struck almost dumb. One more dear little feeble child I am to meet no more till the dead small & great shall stand before God. This is a bitter cup indeed, but blessed be God . . ."

He cautioned the family not "to cast an unreasonable blame on my dear Ruth on account of the dreadful trial we are called [to] suffer. . . ." And to Mary, he said, "If I had a right sence of my habitual neglect of my familys Eternal interests; I should probably go crazy."

A few days later, still feeling guilty about not being with them, he assured Mary that "any ideas that *to me* the separation is not a painful one are wholly mistaken ones. . . . When the day *comes* that will afford me an opportunity to return I shall be awake to greet the earliest dawn; if not its *midnight birth*."

In the summer of 1847, Mary and most of the rest of the family joined Brown in Springfield. He continued to work long hours, but his attention — like that of the nation — was increasingly drawn to Texas and the issue of slavery.

Texas had been part of Mexico until 1836, when American settlers, mostly from the slaveholding South, revolted and set up an independent, slaveholding nation: the Republic of Texas.

Mexico refused to relinquish its claim to the territory, however, and in 1845 the United States went to war.

Many Americans opposed the war as illegal and immoral, including Abraham Lincoln, who believed the United States had forced the war on Mexico to seize more territory for slave owners.

Future president Ulysses S. Grant, who served as a captain in the war, later wrote: "I had a horror of the Mexican War . . . only I had not moral courage enough to resign. . . ."

The United States defeated Mexico and gained undisputed title to Texas, California, New Mexico, Utah, Nevada, Arizona, and parts of Colorado and Wyoming. Southern members of Congress urged the South to unite so slavery could expand to the new territories, while every Northern state except Iowa passed legislation demanding that Congress exclude slavery from the new territories.

In his final act as a congressman, John Quincy Adams voted a resounding "No!" to legislation awarding medals to American officers who fought in the war. Seconds later, the last battle in his long struggle against slavery over, he slumped unconscious in his seat. Two days later he died.

John Brown was appalled at the possibility that the American slave empire might soon stretch from the Atlantic to the Pacific. Impatient with the largely verbal opposition to slavery of many white abolitionists, he reached out to black abolitionists who believed in

fighting slavery with deeds — men like Underground
Railroad conductor and ex-slave Henry Highland
Garnet: a clergyman, abolitionist, and editor whose
sister had been kidnapped in New York City and sold
into slavery.

Garnet roamed the streets for days afterwards
holding an open knife in his pocket, hoping slave
catchers would try to seize him so he could kill them.
But none tried, and he never saw his sister again.

Most of all, Brown wanted to meet Frederick
Douglass. In the years since his escape from slavery,
Douglass had become the leading spokesman for

*Henry Highland Garnet, an underground railroad conductor and
ex-slave.*

black Americans, braving mobs that stoned, beat, and sometimes tried to kill him as he traveled throughout the North delivering antislavery lectures.

In November, 1847, Brown invited the thirty-year-old Douglass to his home in Springfield. "A small, wooden building on a back street in a neighborhood of laboring men, . . ." said Douglass. "There was an air of plainness about it which almost suggested destitution."

Every member of the family made him welcome and they all sat down to eat. Then afterwards, while the sons cleared the table and washed the dishes, Brown began to tell of his plan to end slavery.

"Slavery was a state of war," Douglass recalled Brown saying, and "the slaves had the right to gain their liberty in any way they could . . ."

But Douglass said Brown's plan "did not, as some might suppose, contemplate a general rising among the slaves, and a general slaughter of the slave masters. An insurrection, he thought, would only defeat the object . . ."

Instead, Brown proposed creating a guerilla force that would gradually undermine slavery by destroying "the money value of slave property, and that can only be done by rendering such property insecure."

He brought out a map of the United States and drew Douglass's attention to the Allegheny Mountains, stretching from Pennsylvania down through Maryland and Virginia.

"These mountains are the basis of my plan," he said. "God has given the strength of the hills to freedom; they were placed here for the emancipation of the Negro race; they are full of natural forts, where one man for defense will be equal to a hundred for attack. . . . My plan, then, is to take at first about twenty-five picked men. . . . The most persuasive and judicious of these shall go down to the fields from time to time, as opportunity offers, and induce the slaves to join them, seeking and selecting the most restless and daring."

Once he had "one hundred hardy men," the plan would "begin in earnest; they would run off the slaves in large numbers, retain the strong and brave ones in the mountains, and send the weak and timid to the North by the Underground Railroad. His operations would be enlarged with increasing numbers and would not be confined to one locality."

When Douglass objected that such a plan would only make Virginia slave owners sell their slaves farther south, Brown replied: "That will be what I want first to do. . . . If we could drive slavery out of *one county*, it would be a great gain — it would weaken the system throughout the state."

He believed that slavery could be driven all the way to the Gulf states, and then abolished by public sentiment.

The two talked from eight in the evening till three in the morning, with Brown trying to overcome

Frederick Douglass traveled extensively, giving antislavery lectures.

Douglass's objections: the difficulty of supplying the men with food and ammunition, the bloodhounds that would be used to hunt them down, the unrelenting force that would be hurled against them by slave owners, state governments, and the government of the United States.

Finally, as they both grew weary, Brown said that even if the plan failed, "he had no better use for his life than to lay it down in the cause of the slave."

Long afterwards Douglass declared, "I have talked with many men, but I remember none, who seemed so deeply excited upon the subject of slavery as he.

He would walk the room in agitation at the mention of the word."

Brown failed to persuade Douglass, who feared that failure would lead to bloody reprisals against black people throughout the United States.

Brown continued to spend long hours in his wool business, but found time in the fall of 1848 to travel to New York's Adirondack Mountains to visit a community of black settlers near the village of North Elba. Mary and their newest child, five-month-old Ellen, traveled with him as far as Whitehall, New York, where they visited Mary's brother.

The settlers were living on land donated by Gerrit Smith, a wealthy, upstate New York abolitionist who hated slavery as much as Brown did, and the two liked each other immediately. The pioneer conditions reminded Brown of his youth in the Western Reserve, and he talked about moving to North Elba to teach the settlers how to farm.

He told Smith he would "be a kind of father to them."

Shortly after returning to Springfield, Brown wrote his father, "I can think of no place where I would sooner go, all things considered, than to live with these despised Africans, to try and encourage them and show them a little — so far as I am capable — of how to manage."

His daughter Ruth said he also saw an opportunity to train some of the men "for the great work. . . ."

On the way home from North Elba, Ellen caught a violent cold, and in the weeks that followed grew steadily worse. Brown still put in long hours almost every day at the warehouse, but his time at home "was mostly spent in caring for her," Ruth said. "He sat up nights to keep an even temperature in the room, and to relieve mother from the constant care which she had through the day. He used to walk with the child and sing to her so much that she soon learned his step."

One day he came home a little before noon, "and looked at her and said, 'She is almost gone.' She heard him speak, opened her eyes, and put up her little wasted hands with such a pleading look for him to take her that he lifted her from the cradle . . . and carried her until she died. He was very calm, closed her eyes, folded her hands, and laid her in her cradle. When she was buried father broke down completely and sobbed like a child. . . ."

When baby Amelia had been scalded to death a few months before, even that deep personal sorrow had turned Brown's thoughts to the plight of slaves.

Her death, he wrote Mary at the time, should make them all "feel the more for vast numbers who are forced away from their dearest relatives with little if any hope of ever meeting them again on this side [of] the grave."

The South had become one huge, armed concentration camp where slaves were forbidden to leave plantations without a pass, men on horseback constantly patrolled the roads, and slaves were still being maimed and killed for attempting to escape.

In a small town in North Carolina, a free black youth named Lewis Sheridan Leary was forced to flee after thrashing a slave owner he saw brutally beating a slave.

"Tell no man where I have gone," he ordered his brother, "and you'll see me again, but I'll be marching at the tap of a drum."

Leary's flight would take him to Oberlin, and eventually, to John Brown. For now, though, Brown's attempts to rescue his faltering wool business carried him to London where he was forced to sell his wool at disastrously low prices.

The struggle against slavery would not let him rest even thousands of miles from home, however, and he made a quick trip to France. There he traveled to the battlefield at Waterloo to study Napoleon's tactics, perhaps dreaming of leading his own army "marching at the tap of a drum."

CHAPTER FOUR

THE STORM

John Brown returned from Europe to find the country torn by the issue of whether to admit California as a free or a slave state. Even while his mind and time were occupied with trying to save the Perkins & Brown wool business, he closely followed the furious debate.

Frightened leaders from both North and South hurriedly worked out a compromise to keep the South from seceding: the Compromise of 1850.

It was meant to appeal to Northerners by admitting California as a free state and prohibiting the slave trade in the nation's capital, where it had always flourished. The compromise was meant to appeal to Southerners by including a new Fugitive Slave Law that required every citizen to help slave owners catch slaves under threat of fine or imprisonment.

The man or woman charged with being a fugitive was denied a jury trial. Their fate was decided by a United States judge or commissioner who was given ten dollars for every person he sent to slavery, but only five dollars if he let the person go free.

Though Brown still lived primarily in Springfield, he had moved his family to North Elba shortly before leaving for Europe.

"It now seems that the Fugitive Slave Law was to be the means of making more Abolitionists than all the lectures we have had for years," he wrote Mary. "I of course keep encouraging my colored friends to 'trust in God and keep their powder dry.'"

As soon as he found time, he traveled to North Elba and "bade us resist any attempt that might be made to take any fugitive from our town," Ruth said, "regardless of fine or imprisonment. . . . Father at this time said, 'Their cup of iniquity is almost full.'"

One evening while Ruth was singing a song called "The Slave Father Mourning for his Children," Brown suddenly said, "Oh Ruth! don't sing any more; it is too sad."

While he was in North Elba, Brown gave words of encouragement to his black neighbors, especially Lyman Epps, who often helped out on the Brown farm.

The Fugitive Slave Law threatened free blacks as well as fugitives, for if they could not produce proof of their freedom whenever any white person demanded it, they could be sold into slavery. Four of

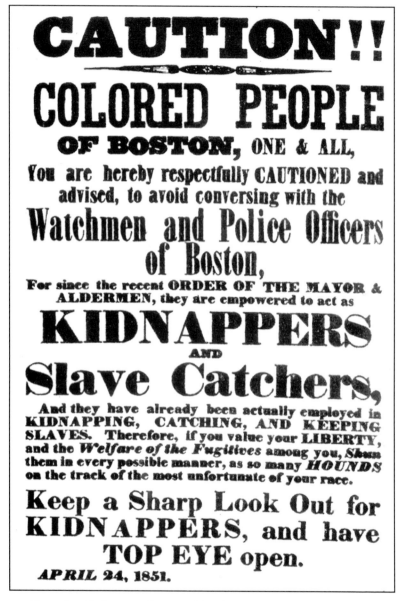

Even free blacks were threatened by the Fugitive Slave Law.

the first eight "slaves" sent into captivity under the new law were later found to be freemen who had been kidnapped.

Hundreds of black families fled to Canada as a reign of terror descended on the black population.

"Many families who had lived in the city for twenty years, fled from it now," said Harriet Jacobs, who had escaped from slavery five years before and now lived in New York City. ". . . many a husband discovered that his wife had fled from slavery years ago, and as 'the child follows the condition of its mother,' the children of his love were liable to be seized and carried to slavery. Everywhere, in those humble homes, there was consternation and anguish."

Brown was forced to return to Springfield and his business worries, even though he was reluctant to leave North Elba.

Never before, he wrote his children, "did the country seem to hold out so many things to entice me to stay on its soil. *Nothing* but the strong sense of duty, Obligation and propriety, would keep me from laying my bones to rest there. . . ."

Within days, he wrote Mary that he was giving his black neighbors "all the encouragement in my power . . . some of them are so alarmed that they tell me they cannot sleep on account of either themselves or their wives and children. I can only say I think I have been enabled to do something to revive their broken spirits. I want all my family to imagine themselves in the same dreadful condition. . . ."

Blacks throughout the North organized to physically resist what they called the "blood-hound" bill, and many whites joined them. Vigilance committees in Philadelphia, Detroit, New York, and other cities signed up both black and white members who vowed to help fugitives at a moment's notice.

In Detroit, black men also formed a secret organization called the African-American Mysteries: The Order of the Men of Oppression, and risked their lives to help escaping slaves.

Committees made up of blacks and whites pledged to help fugitives.

"It was fight and run — danger at every turn," said cofounder William Lambert, "but that we calculated upon, and were prepared for."

But other people, even if they thought the law immoral, refused to oppose it.

"I confess I hate to see the poor creatures hunted down," Abraham Lincoln wrote a friend, "but I bite my lips and keep quiet."

Believing as always that trust in God required action by men and women, Brown helped organize his black friends in Springfield into an armed resistance movement called the United States League of the Gileadites. The name was taken from the Biblical story of Gideon, who chose only the bravest of the brave to fight for the freedom of his people.

Springfield's League of the Gileadites was now an active organization. Three years later, when two thousand United States soldiers were called out in Boston to return fugitive Anthony Burns to slavery, a visitor to Springfield found armed black men posted everywhere in their neighborhood, and women ready with boiling water to scald any slave catchers who came near.

The slave catchers had been there, said black abolitionist William Wells Brown, but "the authorities, foreseeing a serious outbreak, advised them to leave, and . . . these disturbers of the peace had left in the evening train for New York. . . ."

More and more black Americans were proving

they were in earnest about fighting for their rights, and many whites were joining them. The growing struggle against slavery also gained new white adherents with the publication in 1852 of *Uncle Tom's Cabin*.

The novel, which broke all records by selling over three hundred thousand copies in its first year, exposed the evils of slavery to much of the general public for the first time. White Southerners reacted angrily, and a black man in Maryland named Samuel Green was sentenced to ten years in prison after authorities found him with a copy of the book.

Harriet Beecher Stowe, the famous author of Uncle Tom's Cabin.

"The star of hope is slowly and steadily rising above the horizon," Brown wrote Mary. "As one sign of these times I would like to mention the publication of *Uncle Tom's Cabin* . . . which has come down upon the abodes of bondage like the morning sunlight unfolding . . . in a manner which has awakened a sympathy for the slave in hearts unused to feel. . . ."

Perkins & Brown had finally gone out of business, but most of Brown's time was taken up with trying to settle the numerous lawsuits brought against him in connection with the wool business.

He moved his family back to Akron, where he planned to remain only long enough to wind up his partnership with Perkins. (Ruth, who had married a local farmer named Henry Thompson, remained in North Elba.) The lawsuits dragged on, however, forcing him to travel back and forth to the East to testify in courtrooms in Pittsburgh, New York, Boston, and other cities.

In the spring of 1854, while helping a lawyer prepare a case near Utica, New York, Brown "suddenly turned to his counsel and said, 'I am going to Boston.' 'Going to Boston!' said the astonished lawyer; 'why do you want to go to Boston?' Old Brown continued walking vigorously, and replied, 'Anthony Burns must be released, or I will die in the attempt.' . . . It took a long and earnest talk with old Brown to persuade him to remain."

Finally, all the lawsuits were settled and he began

making plans to move his family back to North Elba, where he dreamed they would live the rest of their lives. But suddenly his plans fell apart because of a bill passed by Congress: the Kansas-Nebraska Act.

In 1820, as part of an effort to resolve a crisis over slavery that threatened to destroy the Union, Missouri was admitted as a slave state and Maine (which had formerly been part of Massachusetts), as a free state. At the same time, Congress agreed that slavery would be prohibited in any future states carved out of territory acquired by the Louisiana Purchase if the states lay north of latitude 36° 30' — basically the huge northern part of the Great Plains.

Thomas Jefferson said the Compromise was "like a fire bell in the night," warning of the possible future destruction of the nation over the issue of slavery.

John Quincy Adams had declared that the bill was "a law for perpetuating slavery in Missouri, and perhaps in North America. . . ."

Agonizing over the effect of slavery on the country and how best to end it, he seemed to be thinking of some future John Brown as he wrote: "Slavery is the great and foul stain upon the North American Union. . . . A life devoted to abolishing it would be nobly spent or sacrificed."

The Missouri Compromise helped hold the Union together for over thirty years, but in 1854, proslavery forces led by Illinois Senator Stephen Douglas —

who wanted to be president and needed the support of the South to achieve his goal — repealed the Compromise.

Instead of admitting Kansas and Nebraska as free states, as the law had called for, Congress now said settlers could make Kansas a slave state if they wanted to. (The future of Nebraska was left to be decided later.)

The reaction of the nation was swift and fierce, with Southerners determined to extend slavery to Kansas and Northerners determined to make it free.

An angry Frederick Douglass declared: "If the Union can only be maintained by new concessions to the slaveholders, if it can only be stuck together and held together by a new drain on the negro's blood, then . . . let the Union perish."

The Kansas-Nebraska Act not only rocked the nation, but sent powerful tremors through John Brown's family. Reverend Samuel Adair, Brown's brother-in-law, moved to Kansas and wanted "good men and true" to follow him there.

Five of Brown's sons — John, Jr., Jason, Owen, Frederick, and Salmon — were struggling as farmers through a drought-stricken Ohio summer, and began to talk about following "Uncle Adair" to Kansas.

"If you or any of my family are disposed to go to Kansas or Nebraska, with a view to help defeat Satan and his legions in that direction," Brown wrote John, Jr., who had asked him to go with them, "I have not a word to say; *but I feel committed to operate in another part of the field. . . ."*

His sons kept trying to persuade him, however, and a few weeks later he wrote Ruth and her husband: "After being hard pressed to go with my family to Kansas as more likely to benefit the colored people *on the whole* than to return with them to North Elba; I have consented to ask for your *advice & feeling* in the matter. . . ."

Brown also asked Frederick Douglass and Gerrit Smith for advice. Douglass apparently never replied, but Smith urged him to return to North Elba and Brown decided to do so.

In the fall of 1854, while Brown was trying to raise money for the move back to North Elba, Owen, Salmon, and Frederick started driving their combined herd of eleven head of cattle toward Kansas and the new homes they hoped to build.

"We sold off all our property and bought blooded cattle, seed, fruit trees, vines and farm implements to take with us," John, Jr., said. ". . . I took a library of four hundred volumes that I had been collecting since I was sixteen. That was, in all probability, the only library in the territory. . . ."

Brown's desire to live the rest of his life in North Elba was probably strengthened by the birth of his and Mary's thirteenth and final child: a daughter they named Ellen in honor of the daughter they had lost.

But by the time John, Jr., and Jason left for Kansas

with their families in the spring of 1855, Brown was seriously thinking of going, too. Whether his change of mind came about primarily because he envisioned being able to start over in a new land, or because he wanted to stop slavery from spreading into that land, he didn't say. But he quickly learned from his sons how violent the struggle to stop slavery was likely to be.

The steamboat his sons took up the Missouri River was crowded with drunken, cursing Southerners armed with bowie knives and guns, boasting they were going to kill all the "damned Abolitionists" or run them out of Kansas.

Jason's four-year-old son, Austin, died of cholera near the village of Waverly, Missouri, about sixty miles from their destination. The families went ashore and "buried him at night . . . our lonely way illuminated only by the lightning of a furious thunder storm," said John, Jr.

"True to his spirit of hatred of Northern people, our captain, without warning to us on shore, cast off his lines and left us to make our way by stage. . . ."

The brothers and their families settled in eastern Kansas in the Pottawatomie Creek region amid rains so heavy, declared Salmon, "sometimes it looked as thou the whole territory was agoing to be drownded."

A few days after their arrival, Jason said, "A squad of Missourians rode up" and asked which side of the slavery question they were on. " 'We are Free State,' we answered, 'and more than that we are Abolitionists.' They rode away at once, and from that moment on we were marked for destruction."

Many other free state settlers had arrived in Kansas in the months before the Brown brothers came, settling mainly in the lands between the Kansas River in the north and Pottawatomie Creek in the south. These settlers were often attacked by armed, proslavery men from Missouri, who carried flags painted with skulls and crossbones, and proudly called themselves "Border Ruffians."

In the spring, Border Ruffians cast more than six thousand illegal votes, and installed a proslavery territorial legislature in the town of Shawnee Mission.

The members of the Shawnee Legislature promptly passed laws permitting only proslavery men to hold office; limiting jury service to those who believed in slavery; making it a crime, punishable by at least five years at hard labor, to say slavery was illegal in Kansas; and requiring imprisonment for anyone helping slaves escape or possessing books dealing with slave resistance or rebellion.

The legislature also effectively barred free state settlers from seeking justice through the law by requiring all sheriffs and judges to be proslavery.

In May, 1855, John, Jr., wrote his father that proslavery men were massing on the Kansas border "to fasten Slavery upon this glorious land by means no matter how foul. . . ."

In a bid for the presidency, Senator Stephen Douglas led the fight for the repeal of the Missouri Compromise.

He declared that antislavery people were disorganized and unarmed, and "should *immediately, thoroughly arm*, and *organize themselves in military companies.* In order to effect this, some persons must begin and lead off in the matter. Here are five men of us who are not only anxious to fully prepare, but are thoroughly determined to fight. . . . Now we want you to get for us these arms. We need them more than we do bread. . . ."

Brown said later that not until he received this letter from John, Jr., did he finally make up his mind to go to Kansas. But though it would take him a while to realize, the letter was the call he had waited for since the day he consecrated his life to the destruction of slavery at the meeting mourning Lovejoy.

Brown soon obtained the arms his sons needed, in part by appealing for donations at an abolitionist convention in Syracuse. Frederick Douglass and Gerrit Smith were there, and they supported him.

Near the end of July, he and Henry Thompson left North Elba on their way to Kansas. Twenty-year-old Watson stayed behind to help Mary and Ruth run the farm.

The parting was hard for all of them and, as Brown was leaving the house, he turned to Mary and his children.

"If it is so painful for us to part with the hope of meeting again," he said, "how dreadful must be the feelings of hundreds of poor slaves who are separated for life."

He and Thompson stopped in Akron, where the townspeople gave them large amounts of clothing, boots, and weapons, including several cases of guns belonging to the state of Ohio.

Brown shipped the weapons to Chicago, where he and Thompson loaded them into a horse-drawn wagon and began the journey toward Kansas. Along the way they picked up sixteen-year-old Oliver, who had been working on a farm in Illinois.

Near Independence, Missouri, he saw a slave pen

"built like a chicken coop, only stronger and higher. Inside the pen was the auction block."

Later, he saw handcuffed black men, women, and children standing on a river bank, waiting to be taken to New Orleans. The sights stirred Brown to the depths of his soul.

And the closer he, Henry, and Oliver came to Kansas, the more danger pressed around them. One day an old man in Missouri, after finding out they were Northerners, warned they'd never reach Kansas alive.

"We are prepared," Brown answered quietly, "not to die alone."

John Brown was now fifty-five, a "clean-shaven, scrupulously neat, well dressed, quiet" man, ready to play his role in the great struggle that was about to begin. Others who had pledged their lives to end slavery were also on the move.

In the East, a black woman in her thirties named Harriet Tubman used the Appalachians — the mountains Brown told Douglass had been put there by God "for the emancipation of the Negro race" — as an escape route for slaves.

She had escaped from slavery several years before and now returned time and again to rescue others. Her path and that of John Brown would one day cross.

In Virginia, a quiet, twenty year old named John

Reverend Samuel Adair, John Brown's brother-in-law.

Henri Kagi, a descendant of Swiss Mennonites who settled in Shenandoah County, was forced to quit teaching school and leave the state because of his antislavery views.

Kagi said he was willing to die to end slavery because, he declared, "It steals babes in the cradle . . . robs women of their chastity and men of their wives. It kills . . . more in number than the sword."

Kagi was described by a cousin as having "more the appearance of a divinity student than a warrior," and "kind in his feelings to every one, especially to children, whose confidence he acquired at first acquaintance."

John Henri Kagi's determination to end slavery was about to lead him to Kansas, its rapidly spreading violence, and a fateful meeting with John Brown.

"The storm every day thickens," John, Jr., had written his father several weeks before the latter started for Kansas. "Its near approach is hourly more clearly seen by all. . . . The great drama will open here, when will be presented the great struggle in arms, of Freedom and Despotism in America. . . ."

The storm over slavery feared by so many since the founding of the nation was about to break over the plains of Kansas.

CHAPTER FIVE

BLEEDING KANSAS

The journey west took forty-four days. Brown stopped at Waverly and disinterred the body of Austin so he could take it to the grieving parents.

It was early October before the three men arrived at "Brownsville," the place where John, Jr., and his brothers had staked their claims. It was a fertile stretch of land in the Pottawatomie Creek region of eastern Kansas, a few miles from Reverend Adair's cabin in Osawatomie.

The weary travelers had a total of sixty cents in their pockets, but they had managed to bring the wagonload of weapons safely through hostile Missouri, carefully hidden under Brown's surveying instruments and other possessions.

The land was beautiful, with thick groves of trees along the creek banks and an ocean of grass covering

John Brown's cabin at Osawatomie, Kansas.

the gently sloping prairie, cut here and there by sharp ravines.

But Brown was shocked at what he found. Almost everyone in the family was sick and unable to work, none of the crops had been gathered, no fences built, and untended cattle roamed the fields and gardens, trampling everything in sight.

Worst of all, his sons had been too sick to build cabins, so they and their families were living in makeshift tents, "shivering over their little fires," Brown wrote Mary, "all exposed to the dreadful cutting winds, morning and evening and stormy days. We have been trying to help them all in our power, and hope to get them more comfortable soon."

Jason and Ellen were greatly relieved now that they could bury Austin on their own land and Ellen, who had been so depressed she wanted to return east, agreed to stay.

Brown set to work at once nursing the sick, while Henry and Oliver unloaded the wagon. They erected a tent and placed the weapons inside. That night they all sat around a fire and talked about the latest political developments. John, Jr., told his father that in two days the free staters were going to elect a congressional representative, plus delegates to write a Free State constitution for the Territory.

Hearing that there was "a prospect of difficulty," Brown wrote Mary, "we all turned out most thoroughly armed (except Jason, who was too feeble); but no enemy appeared, nor have I heard of any disturbance in any part of the Territory. Indeed, I believe Missouri is fast becoming discouraged about making Kansas a slave State, and I think the prospect of its becoming free is brightening every day."

Brown would soon learn how wrong he was, but,

for the next several weeks, he was able to concentrate on helping his family prepare for winter.

They built rude shelters with three walls made of prairie grass tied to stakes pounded into the ground, and a fourth side open to the weather. They built a dirt-floored log cabin for Jason and Ellen, and started a cabin for John, Jr., and his family, but freezing weather stopped them before they could finish.

Besides being hampered by illness, the Brown brothers had accomplished little because they spent so much time trying to save the Territory from slavery.

"Our men have so much of war and elections to attend to," Ellen wrote her mother, "that it seems as though we were a great while getting into a house."

Brown seemed to feel guilty about leaving Mary to struggle without him in the cold of North Elba, and wrote her that "those here are not altogether in paradise" either.

A few miles south of Brownsville was the tiny settlement of Shermanville. Several proslavery people lived there, including "Dutch Henry" Sherman and Pleasant Doyle, who sometimes gave the Border Ruffians the names of free state settlers to intimidate or kill.

The Shermanville people let it be known they considered the Browns free state ringleaders who would one day have to be dealt with by the Ruffians and their allies.

Brown also discovered to his dismay that many of the free staters were as antiblack as the proslavery people.

Just a few weeks before Brown's arrival, leaders of the newly formed Free State Party passed a platform condemning abolitionists and declaring that "the best interests of Kansas require a population of free white men, and . . . we are in favor of stringent laws, excluding all negroes, bond or free, from the Territory. . . ."

Brown attended a meeting in Osawatomie, where he rose to reply to their antiblack sentiments "and soon alarmed and disgusted" those present by "asserting the manhood of the negro race, and expressing his earnest, anti-slavery convictions with . . . force and vehemence . . ."

Despite the antiblack sentiments of many free staters, however, they were determined to form a state government in opposition to the proslavery Shawnee Legislature. President Franklin Pierce called their efforts "treasonable insurrection" and warned he would use the United States Army to crush them if necessary.

Stephen Douglas went even further, and called on Pierce to hang the free state leaders as traitors.

Near the end of October, a settler was murdered by a proslavery man, but authorities made no attempt to arrest the killer. In November, near Lawrence (which Border Ruffians called an "Abolitionist nest"), a free state settler from Ohio was murdered by a Virginian. The next night the only witness to the murder — a man named Jacob Branson — was arrested by the sheriff so he could not testify against the killer.

A free state posse quickly rescued Branson, leading the sheriff to warn Governor Wilson Shannon that an armed force was operating in Lawrence in "open rebellion against the laws of the Territory."

The governor called out the proslavery militia, and Atchison came in from Missouri with hundreds of Border Ruffians vowing to kill the abolitionist "outlaws."

Brown immediately sent John, Jr., toward Lawrence on horseback when he heard the news, intending to wait until the next day to go himself.

"But before he had gone many rods," Brown wrote his wife, "word came that our help was immediatley wanted. On getting this last news, it was at once agreed . . . that all the men but Henry, Jason, and Oliver should at once set off for Lawrence under arms; these three being wholly unfit for duty."

They loaded the wagon with guns, ammunition, and supplies, and started for Lawrence in the late afternoon. Brown also took several poles with fixed bayonets, ready for instant use. About three miles outside Lawrence, they came to a bridge held by proslavery men.

Everyone in the Brown party had a heavy sword strapped to his body and "a gun, with two large revolvers in a belt exposed to view, with a third in his pocket," Brown told Mary, "and as we moved directly on to the bridge without making any halt, they for some reason suffered us to pass without interruption. . . ."

Brown found Lawrence full of companies of militia drilling behind earthworks the citizens had just finished erecting, and the streets teeming with people fearing an attack at any moment. Brown was commissioned a captain and John, Jr., a lieutenant in the Liberty Guards, the Osawatomie company of the First Brigade of Kansas Volunteers.

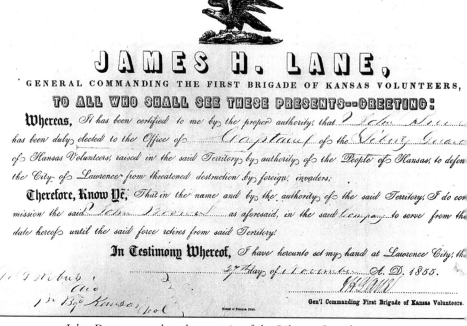

John Brown was elected a captain of the Liberty Guards.

Governor Shannon, with a force of close to two thousand camped on the banks of the Wakarusa River outside town, had already expressed a willingness to end the crisis peacefully. Shannon and other proslavery leaders were willing to talk because they feared the increasingly violent behavior of their own men, whom the governor called a "pack of hyenas."

The crisis ended with Shannon signing a document giving the free staters everything they asked for, prompting Brown to write Mary: "Free State men have only hereafter to retain the footing they have gained, and *Kansas is free.*"

Before Brown left Lawrence, he sought out a man named James F. Legate, who had lived in the South for several years, and asked him many questions about slaves. Brown especially wanted to know if the slaves would fight for their freedom if the opportunity arose.

Legate's reply is not known, but in the months the free staters were fighting to stop slavery from coming into Kansas, slaves throughout the South were risking their lives for freedom.

In a large swamp in North Carolina, according to a letter from several white citizens to the governor, runaway black men, women, and children had planted gardens, built shelters, and were living lives of freedom in defiance of all attempts to recapture them.

They were "dangerous to all persons living by or near said swamp," the whites complained, and when attacked by the slaveholders, killed one of them and "ran off cursing and swearing and telling them to come on, they were ready for them again."

No slave hunters could be found willing to go into the swamp after them, however.

Increasing numbers of people were also violating the Fugitive Slave Law, including members of a black vigilance committee in Cleveland who helped 275 fugitives escape in eight months.

The federal district attorney in Massachusetts urged that Reverend Theodore Parker and other abolitionists who violated the Law be charged with treason, declaring that whoever violated it "must risk hanging for it."

Brown, his sons, and other free staters were also being called traitors by federal officials and by Stephen Douglas, who called on President Pierce to hang all their leaders in Kansas.

Brown could not have cared less about being called a traitor by men who supported slavery, and proudly told Ruth the conduct of the defenders of Lawrence fully sustained "the high character of the Revolutionary fathers."

The winter passed quietly, although in January President Pierce yielded to the pleas of Governor Shannon and Secretary of War Jefferson Davis — a slaveholder who was later to become president of the Confederacy — to declare the Shawnee Legislature legal.

Through most of the winter, however, men and women were more preoccupied with the bitter weather than with the threats of proslavery leaders.

"Thermometer on Sunday and Monday at twenty-eight to twenty-nine below zero, . . ." Brown wrote Mary. "Oliver was laid up by freezing his toes . . . He will be crippled for some days yet. Owen has one foot some frozen. We have middling tough times (as some would call them). . . . All mail communications are entirely cut off by the snowdrifts. . . ."

He also told his wife he missed her so much: "I seldom allow my thoughts to dwell upon it. . . . Suffice it to say, that God is *abundantly* able to keep both us and you, and in him let us all trust."

As spring drew near, Brown worried the United States Army would be used against antislavery settlers. President Pierce had already placed the soldiers of Fort Riley and Fort Leavenworth at the disposal of Governor Shannon.

"The President never will *dare* employ the troops of the United States to shoot the citizens of Kansas," Ohio Congressman Joshua Giddings replied to a letter from Brown. "The death of the first man by the troops will involve every free State in your own fate. *It will light up the fires of civil war throughout the North, and we shall stand or fall with you. . . .*"

But Giddings was wrong, as Brown and the other free staters would soon find out.

Spring came, and with it more proslavery men. In April, a man from Alabama named Jefferson Buford rode into Kansas with four hundred armed Southerners. Many carried banners reading "*The Supremacy of the White Race.*"

A company of Buford's men camped on Pottawatomie Creek, only about two miles from the Browns.

Brown heard that some of the men camped on the Pottawatomie "were coming to the cabin that my son and I were staying in . . . to set fire to it and shoot us as we ran out. Now, that was not proof enough for me; but I thought I would satisfy myself, and if they had committed murder in their hearts, I would be justified in killing them."

So he disguised himself as a surveyor appointed by the Pierce administration and pretended to survey the lands near the men.

"You have a fine country here," he told one of them, "great pity there are so many Abolitionists in it."

"Yes," the man replied, "but by God we will soon clean them all out."

Then Brown said, "I hear there are some bad men about here by the name of Brown."

"Yes, there are," the Southerner replied, "but . . . we will kill them."

Pretending to write down figures from his surveying instruments in a little notebook, Brown instead wrote down every remark made by the men.

Now the Browns knew "that our family were marked for destruction," John, Jr. declared.

The Southerners had also named other potential victims, and Brown warned them. Soon the Osawatomie settlers held a secret meeting to decide what to do. Other secret meetings were held throughout Kansas as free state people realized the government would not protect them, and they would have to protect themselves.

From Chicago to Boston, crowds at mass meetings contributed money to send supplies and antislavery settlers to Kansas. In Brooklyn, the Reverend Henry Ward Beecher used the money he raised to buy Sharpe rifles, declaring they would do more to save Kansas spiritually than Bibles.

On May 8, a whiskey-drinking grand jury under U.S. District Judge S.D. Lecompte indicted several Free State leaders for "high treason," indicted the *Herald of Freedom* newspaper for seditious language because of its antislavery writings, and even indicted two structures: the Free State Hotel in Lawrence, which had been fortified to withstand mob attacks, and a bridge built by Northern settlers.

Three days later, using the pretext that a deputy marshal had been attacked in Lawrence, U.S. Marshal J.B. Donaldson called for all "law-abiding citizens of the Territory" to form an armed posse to enforce "law and order" in the town.

Once more, armed mobs rode into Kansas from

Missouri, joining Buford's men and the other pro-slavers already there, vowing to wipe out the "freedom-shriekers" in Lawrence and elsewhere.

Free state men began to mobilize throughout Kansas. John, Jr., put his Pottawatomie Rifles (the re-formed Liberty Guards) on alert, while Brown organized his unmarried sons and Henry Thompson into "a little company by ourselves."

On May 19, 1856, a young, married, free state settler named Jones was shot in the back and killed by a United States deputy marshal while walking away from a store.

Several hours later, three young free staters rode after the murderers, catching up to them about a mile south of Lawrence.

"Where are you going, gentlemen?" one of the three asked.

"We're going to Franklin and you're going to hell!" the deputy marshal shouted, firing a bullet into his brain.

"A Guerilla war exists in Kansas," declared a man in Leavenworth in response to this and other incidents, "and unless the people in the (Northern) States come to our rescue and relief speedily, we shall all likewise perish."

Then suddenly, during the last half of May, "Bleeding Kansas" exploded.

On May 21, a messenger raced up to Brownsville

on horseback, shouting, "A proslavery army has con-
centrated outside Lawrence, and they have cannon!
Send help at once!"

The Browns and their neighbors started off almost
immediately. But soon after midnight, another messenger intercepted them and told them the Border
Ruffians had taken Lawrence without a fight and
were leveling it with cannon fire.

Though Brown was stunned, he urged the men to
keep marching to Lawrence, but soon another messenger came and said strong proslavery forces had
taken control of the road ahead.

The party decided to camp for the night, a move
Brown considered cowardly, but most of the others
refused to go on without reinforcements. And then
another messenger brought news that stunned them
even more, as it stunned people throughout the North.

Senator Charles Sumner of Massachusetts, an abolitionist who denounced the federal government's
support of proslavery forces in Kansas, had been
beaten almost to death in the Senate by a congressman from South Carolina.

The act infuriated Northerners, and many businessmen, academic leaders, and ordinary citizens talked
of revolution against the United States government.

When the Browns and their friends heard the
news at their camp on the banks of Ottawa Creek,
said Salmon, his father and brothers "went crazy —

SOUTHERN CHIVALRY — ARGUMENT versus CLUB'S.

Senator Charles Sumner was attacked by Congressman Preston Brooks in the Senate.

crazy. . . . It seemed to be the finishing, decisive touch."

Brown called a meeting and said, "Something must be done to show these barbarians that we, too, have rights."

And then he asked for volunteers for a "secret mission."

One of the men said he hoped Brown was going to act with caution, leading Brown to explode, "Caution, caution, sir! I am eternally tired of hearing that word caution. It is nothing but the word of cowardice."

Just as they were about to break camp, a boy came riding up and said the Brown women had been forced to leave home by the Doyles, Dutch Henry, Allen Wilkerson, and others. The women, hastily packing, were heading for Reverend Adair's.

"We . . . returned to find our own homes destroyed, our families shelterless on the prairie, our cattle driven off," John, Jr., remembered. "My books had been burned. A reign of terrorism was on. Organized and armed desperadoes from Missouri, enrolled as deputy United States marshals, and backed by government troops, swarmed over the Territory. To fire on one of them, even in self-defense, was treason."

It was time to "fight fire with fire," John Brown declared, adding, "better that a score of bad men should die than that one man who came here to make Kansas a Free State should be driven out."

Two nights later, he led Owen, Frederick, Salmon, Oliver, Henry Thompson, and two neighbors toward the Doyles' cabin on the Pottawatomie. While Frederick and the neighbors stood guard on the road, Brown burst into the cabin and told the startled occupants the Northern Army had come.

Salmon said that when his father ordered Doyle and his three sons outside, Mrs. Doyle screamed at her husband and sons: "Haven't I told you what you were going to get for the course you have been taking?"

Brown spared the youngest son, but ordered Doyle and the other two sons out into the windy darkness. There, at a signal from him, they were stabbed or hacked to death.

Brown and his war party then moved on to Allen Wilkinson's cabin a half mile away, led him into the darkness, and killed him.

Their last stop was a cabin owned by Dutch Henry. He wasn't there, but his brother was. There were also two travelers staying the night. Brown asked if they had been involved in the attack on Lawrence or had ever aided Border Ruffians. They answered no and he let them go.

But William Sherman was taken outside on Brown's orders and killed.

The killings of antislavery people had been going on for years with little or no interference from authorities, but the killings of the five proslavery men ignited a firestorm of action by state and federal officials.

Arrest warrants charging murder were sworn out for Brown, his sons, and followers, who took to the bush and began to live as guerrilla fighters, just as many other free state men were now doing. Warrants charging treason against the United States were issued for John, Jr., and Jason, who had not taken part in the Pottawatomie killings and were, in fact, critical of them.

Jason was captured by Border Ruffians, who put a noose around his neck and were about to lynch him when an old man successfully pleaded for his life. John, Jr., was captured by United States cavalrymen while hiding in the woods behind Reverend Adair's cabin.

"When I was captured," he said years later, "Captain Walker of the United States cavalry himself tied my arms behind my back with a heavy rope. The rope was held by a sergeant, and I was driven, in front of trotting cavalry, nine miles in the blazing sun to Osawatomie. When the rope was taken off twenty-seven hours later, my arms were swollen as big as my body and had turned black. Rings of skin came off with the ropes — slavery's bracelets. I still wear them."

When he died forty years later, his children found the marks of the rope still on him.

Jason and John, Jr., were chained together at Osawatomie and driven past the cabin of Reverend Adair and Florilla, who ran out to give them a little food.

"What does this mean in this land of the Free," she

demanded of the soldiers, "that you drive these men like cattle and slaves?"

Brown managed to have a note delivered to his sons' captors saying: "I am aware that you hold my two sons, John and Jason, prisoners — John Brown."

Brown was now such a figure of dread to the proslavery forces that the fear inspired by the note probably saved his sons' lives.

Jason and John, Jr., were imprisoned in Fort Leavenworth, where John, Jr., "was a raving maniac, chained to the floor, and ill of some wasting fever for a long time."

Brown and his followers hid in heavy timber along Ottawa Creek while Border Ruffians searched for them.

"The Browns were hunted as we hunt wolves today," one man recalled years later.

Finally, the Ruffians, commanded by Captain Henry Pate of the Missouri militia, went into camp at a place called Black Jack. Nearby settlers, who had been robbed and terrorized by the Ruffians, asked Brown for help in fighting them, and he agreed.

On the morning of June 2, he attacked. The battle raged for two hours when Pate, not knowing that casualties and desertions by the settlers had reduced Brown's forces to a handful, came forward carrying a flag of truce.

Pate said he was a deputy United States marshal

acting under orders of "the Government," looking for "certain persons" who had been indicted. When Pate refused Brown's order to surrender, Brown drew his revolver.

"I had no alternative but to submit, or run and be shot," Pate said. "Had I known who I was fighting, I would not have trusted to a white flag."

Brown's name became a symbol for free staters to rally around after the victory at Black Jack, and he proudly told his wife it was "the first regular battle fought between Free State and proslavery men in Kansas. May God still gird our loins and hold our right hands, and to him we give the glory!"

Guerrilla war now swept the Territory, but Brown and his small army were forced to retreat to the brush again where, he told Mary, "we have, like David of old, had our dwelling with the serpants of the rocks & wild beasts of the wilderness; being obliged to hide away from our enemies."

The free state legislature was scheduled to meet in Topeka on the Fourth of July, and proslavery authorities in Kansas and Washington threatened to break up the gathering.

Brown decided to attend the convention, hoping the free staters would "resist all who should interfere with it, and fight, if necessary, even the United States troops."

But he was disappointed and angry when the free

state legislators quietly dispersed at the command of a United States colonel backed by five companies of soldiers.

The breaking up of the legislature was the final straw for Owen, Salmon, Oliver, and Henry, who decided to leave Kansas.

All spring and summer, proslavery forces had been building a line of forts to be used as bases for terrorizing Northern settlers, and now the federal government had also taken away what little political power the Northerners possessed.

In early August, a weary Brown escorted his sons and Henry to the Nebraska border in an old covered wagon hauled by oxen. All of them were sick with fever and lay inside, while Brown and Frederick walked beside the wagon.

Along the way they passed a band of armed free staters who recognized him and cheered.

"He turned from his ox team and glanced at our party from time to time as we were passing him," said one of them. "No doubt it was a pleasing sight for him to see men in armed opposition to the Slave Power."

In August, bands of free state guerrillas attacked and destroyed one blockhouse after another: New Georgia on August 5th; Franklin on August 14th; Fort Saunders on the 15th; and Fort Titus on the 16th.

The Missourians, desperate to save their dying

cause, invaded Kansas with a force of almost two thousand men under the command of Atchison and John Reid, both generals in the Missouri militia.

"Let no one stay away," read one of their recruiting circulars. "We need the old men to advise, the young to execute."

The largest part of the army headed for Lawrence, while two hundred fifty men under Reid rode toward Osawatomie. They planned to burn both towns, as well as other free state settlements.

Brown (along with Jason, who had been released from prison) arrived at Osawatomie the last week in

Border Ruffians on the way to burn the town of Lawrence, Kansas.

August, planning to fight the Border Ruffians in the area.

On August 29, Frederick and several other messengers raced in from Lawrence, asking for help in defending the town. Brown said he would leave in the morning, and then camped on the heights above the Osage River just north of Osawatomie. He had about fourteen or fifteen new recruits with him, and was unaware that Reid's force was headed for Osawatomie.

The Missourians struck at dawn, and Frederick was their first victim. He had stabled several horses at his uncle Adair's, and was on his way to tend them when he met the raiders.

In the lead was a proslavery minister named Martin White, who reined in his horse and shouted "Halt!"

"Good morning. I think I know you," Frederick replied, and walked toward him.

"I know you, & we are foes," Martin shouted.

Then he raised his gun and shot Frederick through the heart, killing him instantly. Adair's son leaped on a pony and raced into Brown's camp three miles away.

"The Border Ruffians are coming and have killed cousin Frederick," he cried.

"Men, come on," was Brown's only comment, "we must meet them before we get to town."

When one of the recruits asked for instructions about how to behave under fire, Brown told him, "Take more care to end life well than to live long."

He placed his men and about fifteen others who

joined them in heavy timber along the river. The Missourians charged with guns firing and the cannon blasting away with volleys of grapeshot.

Brown, with Jason at his side, rallied his men and they stopped the charge, but the Missourians regrouped and came again. Finally, almost out of ammunition and about to be surrounded, he waded the river with Jason and several others.

One man said Brown looked a "queer figure, in a broad straw hat and a white linen duster, his old coat-tails floating outspread upon the water and a revolver held high in each hand, over his head."

He and Jason set out toward Reverend Adair's cabin when suddenly Jason pointed at a column of smoke rising from Osawatomie.

"God sees it," Brown said, tears running down his face as he realized the Ruffians were burning the town. "I have only a short time to live — only one death to die, and I will die fighting for this cause. There will be no more peace in this land until slavery is done for."

He and Jason watched the burning a while longer, then went to look for Frederick's body.

Brown's actions that day won him the nickname of "Osawatomie" Brown, a name thereafter spoken with admiration and respect by those opposed to slavery, and fear and anger by those who favored it.

The struggle against extending slavery to Kansas was now almost won, though few realized it. The newly-formed Republican Party had emerged with a single plank in its platform: *Stop the bloody struggle in Kansas; stop the spread of slavery in the territories.*

Political pressures forced President Pierce to appoint a new governor, who quickly decided to disband all unlawful fighting forces, including the Border Ruffians. He also ordered the release of John, Jr., from prison.

John Brown was now fifty-six, and was ready to leave Kansas. The clean-shaven, brown-haired farmer and merchant who had come west to help his family, was now a gaunt-looking guerrilla fighter sometimes referred to as the "Old Man."

"His hair and beard grew long and wild, and turned grey," John, Jr., said. "This made him look very strange to us, for he never wore a beard at all until he went to Kansas."

But though the struggle had weakened him physically, it had turned his resolve to destroy slavery into iron.

In early October he headed back east where men and women were still risking prison to defy the Fugitive Slave Law, and many black fugitives were showing they preferred death to a return to slavery.

"There was one of two things I had a *right* to," declared Harriet Tubman, "liberty, or death; if I could not have one, I would have the other; for no man should take me alive. . . ."

So horrible was slavery that some black women tried to kill their babies at birth rather than have them grow up as slaves. (Nat Turner's mother had to be tied down to keep her from killing him when he was born.)

In Cincinnati, Ohio, in 1856, an escaped slave named Simon Garner tried to protect his family when slave catchers broke into the home where they were hiding.

His wife, Margaret, "seeing that their hopes of freedom were in vain, seized a butcher knife that lay on the table and with one stroke cut the throat of her little daughter," a child described by a reporter as "almost white, a little girl of rare beauty." Margaret Garner then said "she had killed one and would like to kill the three others, rather than see them again reduced to slavery."

She and her small children were seized, handcuffed, and put on a ship to be taken back to slavery, but the ship met with an accident and one of the children drowned.

Margaret Garner, said a witness, "displayed frantic joy when told that her child was drowned." A few months later she died, and her husband told a friend "she had escaped at last."

Slavery and freedom, said Abraham Lincoln when the Kansas-Nebraska Act was passed, "are like two wild beasts in sight of each other, but chained and held apart. Some day these deadly antagonists will one or the other break their bonds, and then the question will be settled."

John Brown believed that the time for breaking bonds and settling questions was now: that the suffering and pain of those held in bondage for over two hundred years could no longer be endured by people who claimed to believe in God and freedom.

Soon he would see his friend Frederick Douglass again in Rochester, New York, and meet a young friend of Douglass's named Shields Greene, who had escaped from slavery in South Carolina.

People called Greene "Emperor" because of his royal bearing. He was uneducated and rarely spoke, but brooded much about those still in slavery, especially the son he had left behind.

Like Brown, he was also obsessed with freeing the slaves — an obsession that would one day lead him to a life-changing meeting with the "Old Man" in a Pennsylvania quarry.

For now, though, the two knew nothing of each other as the wagon carrying Brown creaked slowly out of Kansas toward Rochester, Springfield, Boston, and history.

CHAPTER SIX

WHO CAN BE AGAINST US?

The storm over slavery that had swept Kansas now seemed about to break over the rest of the country. Violence or talk of violence was everywhere, including the halls of Congress.

In Boston, where Brown arrived by train in January, 1857, many antislavery people felt the proslavery forces had grown so powerful they could never be defeated.

They would have been even more discouraged had they known Southern senators were secretly urging Jefferson Davis to transfer the army's best weapons to Southern arsenals for use against the North if war should come.

Thomas Wentworth Higginson, a Unitarian minister in Worcester, Massachusetts, who would soon become one of Brown's strongest supporters, said "the [slave] power . . . stands with all the patronage of the greatest nation of the world in its clutches, and with the firmest financial basis in the world . . . if this power be weak, where on wide earth will you look for anything strong?"

Far from despairing at the strength of that power, however, Brown seemed more determined than ever to crush it.

On his way east he stopped in Ohio and visited his half-brother, Jeremiah Brown, who said afterwards: "Since the trouble growing out of the settlement of the Kansas Territory, I have observed a marked change in brother John. Previous to this, he devoted himself entirely to business; but since these troubles he has abandoned all business, and has become wholly absorbed by the subject of slavery. . . . I urged him to go home . . . that I feared his course would prove his destruction and that of his boys. . . . He replied that . . . he knew that he was in the line of his duty, and he must pursue it, though it should destroy him and his family."

Brown embarked on a dizzying round of travel and speech making, trying to raise funds to arm, equip, clothe, and feed men to defend freedom in Kansas.

"God protects us in winter," he told the Massachusetts legislature, "but when the grass gets high enough to feed the horses of the Border Ruffians we may have trouble, and should be prepared for the worst."

The legislators gave him nothing, but the Massachusetts State Kansas Committee promised him two hundred Sharpe rifles, which were already in Tabor, Iowa. He also received many promises of money, but the money itself was slow in coming.

The head of the committee, twenty-five-year-old Franklin Sanborn, a teacher who had opened his own school, introduced Brown to a prominent group of antislavery men: Higginson, who would go on to lead the first black regiment in the Civil War; Reverend Theodore ("Thunder and Lightning") Parker of Boston, the most eloquent and controversial Unitarian minister of his day; Dr. Samuel G. Howe, who had helped a dozen fugitives escape through Boston and coedited an abolitionist paper with his wife, Julia Ward Howe; and George Luther Stearns, a wealthy Boston merchant.

Along with Sanborn and Gerrit Smith, these men would become known as the Secret Six and provide Brown with crucial aid in the months ahead.

Brown also visited Senator Sumner, who was still limping painfully from the beating he had suffered in the Senate. At Brown's request, Sumner showed him the coat he had been wearing the day of the beating.

It was stiff from dried blood and, as Brown held it, staring silently, "his lips compressed and his eyes shown like polished steel."

Brown had not seen Mary and his daughters for a year and a half, so he hurried up to North Elba.

Julia Ward Howe coedited an abolitionist newspaper with her husband, Dr. Samuel G. Howe.

Owen, Oliver, and Watson were there, and Ruth and Henry came over from their nearby farm. Brown felt he could spare only the one night away from his efforts to raise funds.

That evening while the family sat talking before the fireplace, he called two-year-old Ellen to sit on his knee. She refused, afraid of this intense stranger, so he told thirteen-year-old Annie to sit with her.

With Annie on one knee and Ellen on the other, and the fierce winds howling outside, Brown once again sang his favorite hymn:

"Blow ye the trumpet, blow!

"The gladly solemn sound . . ."

The next morning he left his family and the farm, on his way to give speeches in New York City, Syracuse, New Haven, Worcester, Springfield, and several towns in Connecticut.

Sanborn convinced him to visit Concord, where social critic and naturalist Henry David Thoreau invited him to lunch, and essayist/poet Ralph Waldo Emerson later joined them. Though both men believed in nonviolence, they were strongly antislavery and were among the almost one hundred townspeople who listened to Brown speak that night.

"In his speech here," Thoreau later commented, "he referred to what his family had suffered in Kansas, without ever giving the least vent to his pent-up fire. It was a volcano with an ordinary chimney-flue."

Emerson called him "the rarest of heroes, a true idealist, with no by-ends of his own."

Both contributed small amounts of money, which was all Brown seemed able to get no matter how many speeches he made.

"I am literally driven to beg," he told one man, "which is very humiliating."

In March, James Buchanan was inaugurated as president, and promptly urged that Kansas be admitted to the Union as a slave state. The power of the proslavery forces now seemed unstoppable, especially after the United States Supreme Court announced its Dred Scott decision the same month.

Dred Scott was a slave whose owner had taken him to Illinois and Wisconsin Territory, where slavery was banned. Scott then sued for freedom for himself; his wife, Harriet; and their two daughters, on the grounds they had gained it once they were taken to free territory.

Chief Justice Roger Taney, a slave owner (as were four other members of the Supreme Court), ruled that no black man, woman, or child could ever be a citizen of the United States or have any rights "which the white man was bound to respect." Taney also ruled that Congress had no power to prohibit slavery anywhere in the country, thus outlawing the Missouri Compromise.

Many abolitionists realized the ruling could lead to legalization of slavery in the North, and some called for their states to break away from the Union to prevent this from happening. They would have been even angrier had they known that Buchanan secretly pressured the court to issue a proslavery ruling.

Brown said the decision marked "a strange change in morals, political as well as Christian, since 1776," and redoubled his efforts to raise money for his small army.

Sometimes Brown showed listeners a bowie knife he had captured from Captain Pate at Black Jack, and said, "Such a blade as this, mounted upon a strong shaft, or handle, would make a cheap and ef-

An 1857 photo of John Brown.

fective weapon. . . . A resolute woman, with such a pike, could defend her cabin door against man or beast."

He arranged to have one thousand such pikes made. The man who made them must have wondered if Brown really intended to give them to one thousand resolute women to defend their cabin doors.

On a trip to New York City, he met a British soldier of fortune named Hugh Forbes and hired him to train his men. It would turn out to be one of Brown's biggest mistakes.

Toward the end of March, Mary wrote saying their sons, with the sole exception of Owen, had resolved to "learn, & practice war no more" in Kansas or anywhere else.

"I have only to say . . . it was not at my solicitation that they engaged in it at the first," he replied angrily, "& that while I may *perhaps* feel no more love of the business than they do; still I think there may be *possibly* in their day that which is more to be dreaded: if such things *do not now exist.*"

Brown had grown discouraged at the amount of money and supplies he had been able to raise. His goal had been thirty thousand dollars but he had received only one thousand dollars. In addition, though, the Massachusetts Committee had pledged thirteen thousand dollars worth of guns and supplies.

While visiting Boston in early April, 1857, Brown received word that "one of 'Uncle Sam's hounds'" was on his track with an arrest warrant for high treason.

Thomas B. Russell, a judge of the Massachusetts Superior Court who was an abolitionist, agreed to hide him until "the track was cold."

"He had the keenest possible sense of humor, and never missed the point of a joke or of a situation," Mrs. Russell recalled. ". . . When he laughed he made not the slightest sound. . . . It was the most curious thing imaginable to see him, in utter silence, rock and quake with mirth."

One day he told Mrs. Russell about the killing of Frederick, and she said, "If I were you, Mr. Brown, I would fight those ruffians as long as I lived."

"That is not a Christian spirit," he replied. "If I thought I had one bit of the spirit of revenge, I would never lift my hand; I do not make war on slaveholders, even when I fight them, but on slavery."

Brown rarely left his room and was always armed with two knives and three pistols.

"He used to take out his two revolvers and repeater every night before going to bed," Judge Russell said, "to make sure of their loads, saying, 'Here are eighteen lives.'"

Often sick from his exposure to the rain and cold in Kansas, and discouraged by his lack of success in raising money, Brown decided it was time to leave.

"I go with a *sad heart*," he wrote a friend, "having failed to secure even the means of equiping; to say nothing of feeding men. I had when I returned no more that I could peril; & could make no further sacrifice, except to go about in the attitude of a beggar; & that I have done, humiliating as it is."

He journeyed to North Elba to see Mary and the children, and stayed almost two weeks.

"The parting with my wife and young children lay heavy upon my heart," he wrote Sanborn. "They were without income, supplies of clothing, provisions, or even a comfortable house to live in or money to provide any such things."

Referring to the marshal's inability to track him down, he proudly told a friend he was going back to Kansas "with Irons *in* rather than *uppon* my hands."

The journey west took several weeks, with Brown often ill with fever or stopping to try and raise money. In Ohio, he found that citizens in Mechanicsburg had fired on a United States marshal and the slave hunting posse he led. In another town, residents arrested a posse and charged them with using unnecessary force.

But the supporters of slavery were determined not only to protect it in this country, but to expand it to other nations. They backed efforts to take over Nicaragua and Cuba and turn them into slave territories.

Major Robert E. Lee, a slave owner who was superintendent of West Point, was offered command of a privately-financed expedition to invade Cuba, but turned it down because he didn't want to resign from the United States Army.

President Buchanan, with the support of slave owners, urged that a military police force be sent to Mexico, with the hope the United States would eventually control or annex the states of Chihuahua and Sonora. Slave owners would then be free to move their slaves into those states.

John Brown was acutely aware of the proslavery forces raging around him, and more determined than ever to move forward with his plans.

While staying in Hudson, he wrote a friend in

Kansas: "There are some half-dozen men I want a visit from in Tabor, Iowa, to come off in the most QUIET WAY. . . . I have some very important matters to confer with some of you about. Let there be *no words* about it."

He signed the letter "James Smith," one of several aliases he would use from now on. ("Shubel — Hebrew for 'captive of God' — Morgan" and "Nelson Hawkins" were others.)

His men were waiting for him in August, 1857, when he finally arrived in Tabor, just a few miles north of the Kansas border. Also waiting for him were the guns and ammunition sent out by the Massachusetts Kansas Committee, including the two hundred Sharpes rifles and four thousand cartridges. They were being stored by antislavery Quakers.

But contrary to Brown's expectations, there was little violence in Kansas. He waited at Tabor for three months for news of raids by the Border Ruffians, but all was quiet.

The Secret Six were impatient at his inaction, especially Higginson. Why didn't Brown strike at the proslavery forces in Kansas? Higginson demanded in a letter to Sanborn.

"He is as ready for a revolution as any other man," Sanborn replied, "and is now on the borders of Kansas, safe from arrest but prepared for action, but he needs money for his present expenses, and *active* support."

Franklin Sanborn was a member of the Secret Six.

Brown waited in Tabor and then, in October, the free staters won an overwhelming victory at the polls, sending a free state man to Congress and capturing thirty-three of the fifty-two seats in the new Kansas legislature.

Brown finally realized the worst of the slavery struggle in Kansas was over, leaving him free to fight slavery someplace else. He immediately began new preparations and, in November, assembled his volunteers.

These included John Henry Kagi, the teacher who had been forced to leave Virginia because of his antislavery views; John E. Cook, the young lawyer who had tried to capture the murderers of the free state settler, Jones, in the Kansas Territory; Charles Plummer Tidd, a native of Maine who journeyed to Kansas to join the free state forces; and William H. Leeman, an eighteen-year-old whose opposition to slavery was so strong that, in 1856 when he was sixteen, he traveled from Maine to Kansas to do battle with the Border Ruffians.

Leeman was homesick for his family, but wrote in one letter: "I feel myself amply repaid for denying myself the pleasure of seeing them by realizing that I have been engaged in a good cause — a noble cause."

Another recruit, Aaron Dwight Stevens, was an ex-United States cavalryman who was a free state leader in Topeka. Once, when a sheriff threatened to arrest him and his comrades for fighting the Border Ruffians, Stevens cried: "We are in the right, and will resist the universe!"

All these recruits would fight with Brown in the months to come, and most would die.

In November, he told his men for the first time that his ultimate goal was not to fight slavery in Kansas, but to strike at it in Virginia and the South. Cook and two other men (Luke Parsons and Richard Realf, who ultimately dropped out), strongly opposed Brown's plan.

"Some warm words passed between him and myself in regard to the plan," said Cook, "which I had supposed was to be confined entirely to Kansas and Missouri. . . . After a good deal of wrangling we consented to go on, as we had not the means to return, and the rest of the party were so anxious that we should go with them."

Forbes continued training the men, but grew increasingly angry at Brown for not giving him more money and authority. Then suddenly, without explanation, he left the group and hurried to the East.

Brown was annoyed, but didn't yet realize how much trouble Forbes would try to cause.

The men spent most of December hauling their military supplies across Iowa to Springdale, an antislavery settlement about fifty miles from the Illinois border. There they were welcomed by Quakers, who rented them a farmhouse for a small fee.

The men spent their days studying, drilling, and shooting at targets. Five nights a week they discussed slavery and other issues at mock legislative sessions, which were often attended by townspeople.

One Sunday afternoon, Brown told their landlord and two other citizens his plans for the future: they were much like those he had revealed to Frederick Douglass twenty years before.

"He had not then decided to attack the armory at Harpers Ferry," the landlord said, "but intended to take some fifty to one hundred men into the hills near the Ferry and remain there until he could get together quite a number of slaves, and then take what conveyances were needed to transport the Negroes and their families to Canada."

Brown said he would continue to return and make such raids until slavery was destroyed.

"I said to him, 'You and your handful of men cannot cope with the whole South.' His reply was, 'I tell you . . . it will be the beginning of the end of slavery.'"

Brown picked up more recruits from his neighbors at Springdale. These included Stewart Taylor, a twenty-two-year-old Canadian who felt his life would be worthless if it wasn't devoted to fighting slavery, and two brothers, eighteen-year-old Barclay and twenty-two-year-old Edwin Coppoc.

The Coppocs were Quakers who had been born in Ohio and, like several of Brown's followers, were proud of the fact that they were descendants of Revolutionary War soldiers who had risked their lives for freedom.

Brown appointed Stevens as drillmaster and left the men in his charge. Then he hurried to Rochester to meet with Frederick Douglass and perfect the plan for fighting slavery in Virginia.

"Whether I shall be permitted to visit you or not this winter or spring, I cannot now say," he wrote "My Dear Wife and Children, Every One," in January, 1858. "The anxiety I feel to see my wife and children once more I am unable to describe."

But then he said the people held in slavery,

"whose 'tears on their cheeks' are ever in my eyes, and whose sighs are ever in my ears, may however prevent my enjoying the happiness I so much desire. But courage, courage, courage! — the great work of my life. . . . I may yet see accomplished (God helping), and be permitted to return, and 'rest at evening.'"

He spent three weeks discussing his plan with Douglass until, Douglass said, "I confess it began to be something of a bore to me."

Shields Green was often at the house, saying little or nothing, but hanging on every word of this white man who seemed to hate slavery as much as he did.

Brown also worked on a constitution for the government he intended to set up in the mountains of Virginia.

In February, 1858, he traveled to the home of Gerrit Smith, to try to raise money from the Secret Six for his Virginia plan. Most of them were too busy to come, and Sanborn represented them.

"We listened until after midnight, proposing objections and raising difficulties," said Sanborn, "but nothing could shake the purpose of the old Puritan."

Brown resumed the discussion the next day, Sanborn remembered, and finally, "As the sun was setting over the snowy hills of the region where we met, I walked for an hour with Gerrit Smith. . . . Mr. Smith restated in his eloquent way the daring propositions of Brown, whose import he understood

Secret Six member Gerrit Smith.

fully; and then said in substance: 'You see how it is: our dear old friend has made up his mind to this course, and cannot be turned from it. We cannot give him up to die alone. . . .'"

Brown said all he needed was eight hundred dollars and when Sanborn protested "the manifest hopelessness of undertaking anything so vast with such slender means," Brown replied: "If God be for us, who can be against us?"

Years later, Sanborn would write: "Without accepting Brown's plans as reasonable, we were prepared to second them merely because they were his."

Smith pledged several hundred dollars and Sanborn promised to seek the rest from the Secret Six.

A month before the meeting with Smith and Sanborn, Brown had asked Ruth if she would spare Henry "if, on a full explanation, Henry could be satisfied that his family might be safe? I would make a similar inquiry of my own dear wife; but I have kept her tumbling here and there over a stormy and tempestuous sea for so many years that I cannot ask her such a question."

Ruth replied that she could not bear the thought of Henry leaving her again, "yet I know I am selfish. When I think of my poor despised sisters [in slavery], that are deprived of both husband and children, I feel deeply for them; and were it not for my little children, I would go almost anywhere with Henry, if by going I could do them any good."

Brown hurried to New York City and Philadelphia to meet with black leaders and gain their support. In Philadelphia, he and John, Jr., met with William Still and other leaders of the Underground Railroad — men who possessed a vast knowledge of escape routes and hiding places in the South. Still and the others gladly shared their knowledge.

Events were moving swiftly now.

Brown began making arrangements for a convention where he could present his constitution to the black community.

In North Elba, Henry Thompson made preparations to join his father-in-law in going "to school" in Virginia, as Ruth earlier described his fighting experiences in Kansas.

In St. Catherines, Ontario, where she was staying temporarily, Harriet Tubman dreamed she saw "the head of an old man with a long white beard, gazing at her, 'wishful like, jes as ef he war gwine to speak to me,' and then two other heads rose up beside him, younger than he — and as she stood looking at them . . . a great crowd of men rushed in and struck down the younger heads, and then the head of the old man, still looking at her so 'wishful!' "

In Chatham, Ontario, a young black printer named Osborne Perry Anderson — described as "well educated, a man of natural dignity" — worked quietly at his trade, sometimes going hungry so he could buy books. He had been born free, but burned with a desire to help those in slavery.

Soon Brown would come to Chatham, and Anderson's life would change forever.

CHAPTER SEVEN

THE FUGITIVES

The slave system John Brown was preparing to attack was now the nation's most powerful economic
force. By the eve of the Civil War, the worth of slaves
alone — not counting the crops and goods they produced — was almost two billion dollars.

Black men, women, and children were still being
bought and sold like cattle. Slave owners even sold
the children they fathered with the black women
they owned, and the number of these half-white,
half-black sons and daughters in slavery numbered in
the tens of thousands.

The price of slaves rose and fell like the stock market, depending on supply and demand.

A healthy woman with a child could bring in eight
hundred dollars on the open market (equal to about
twelve thousand dollars today), and up to two hundred dollars more if the buyer thought she would

bear more children. "Prime" laborers sold for eight hundred dollars to fifteen hundred dollars apiece.

A mother told of returning from an errand to find the woman who owned her "counting a heap of bills in her lap. My little girl kept crying. . . . She pointed to mistress's lap, and said, 'Brother's money! Brother's money!' Oh, then I understood! I said to mistress McKinley, 'Have you sold my boy?' 'Yes, Charity, and I got a great price for him!'"

One man who escaped from slavery described being sold at the same time as a mother who was torn away from her little daughter. "'Don't leave me,

Slave children were often sold away from their parents.

mama — don't leave me,' screamed the child, as her mother was pushed hastily forward. . . . But she cried in vain. Out of the door and into the street we were quickly hurried. Still we could hear her calling to her mother, 'Come back — don't leave me, . . .' until her infant voice grew faint and still more faint . . . and finally was wholly lost."

In April, 1858, Brown traveled to St. Catherines to meet with Harriet Tubman and they liked each other immediately. "He [Harriet] is the most of a *man*, naturally, that I *ever* met with," Brown wrote John, Jr.

He asked her about the Southern escape routes she had taken during her many rescues, and she gladly shared her knowledge with him.

Brown next traveled to other towns in Ontario — Ingersoll, Hamilton, Chatham, and Toronto — talking to black leaders about a secret convention where he would submit his constitution for the black community's approval.

He decided to hold the meeting in Chatham, where about two thousand fugitives lived. They had organized schools, churches, a newspaper, a fire company, a hotel, and several civic organizations. The community even boasted a handful of black doctors and lawyers.

Brown's great hope, said one of the inhabitants, was that his struggle in the South "would be supported by volunteers from Canada, educated and accustomed to self-government."

Brown appeared at the Chatham home of black abolitionist and author Dr. Martin R. Delany one day, looking "like one of the old prophets," and asked for help in setting up the convention. Delany immediately agreed.

During the second week in May, forty-six delegates (including Brown and his twelve followers), gathered secretly to attend the convention. The sessions were held in several places, but the most important ones took place in the black fire station, "No. 3 Engine House."

There, Kagi read the constitution for governing the territory Brown planned to seize. The document covered just about every aspect of daily life, including a provision to establish black churches and schools "as soon as may be," and another provision imposing the death penalty for rape.

Brown even included a section establishing "intelligence offices" to help the separated members of slave families find each other.

There was strong disagreement only once: over a provision saying "our flag shall be the same that our Fathers fought under in the Revolution."

One delegate said the black men who escaped from slavery "would never think of fighting under the hated 'Stars and Stripes.' . . . but Brown said the old flag was good enough for him. . . . That settled the question."

Some delegates also thought no attack should be made until the United States was engaged in war with a foreign power, but Brown angrily replied, "'I would be the last to take advantage of my country in the face of a foreign foe.' He seemed to regard it as a great insult."

Brown "appeared intensely American," said one man, "he never for a moment thought of fighting the United States as such, but simply the defenders of human slavery in the States. Only the ulcer, slavery, was to be cut from the body politic."

Brown was elected commander-in-chief and the constitution was unanimously adopted, along with "A Declaration Of Liberty By The Representatives of The Slave Population Of The United States of America."

He set July 4, 1858, the eighty-second anniversary of this country's Declaration of Independence, for his attack in the South. Harriet Tubman had suggested the date.

A few days after the convention ended, John Cook left for Harpers Ferry to learn as much as he could about the area.

Then, suddenly, Brown received a frantic message from Sanborn disclosing that Forbes had traveled to Washington and betrayed the plan to several politicians.

"Wilson [Senator Henry] . . . and God knows how many more, have heard about the plot," Howe wrote Higginson.

Higginson and Howe wanted to go ahead anyway, but the other members of the Secret Six — afraid they would be investigated and possibly arrested — insisted Brown postpone the attack for a year. They also ordered him back to Kansas, and Brown, who was again almost penniless, was reluctantly forced to go.

He knew he would probably lose the support of the men he met at Chatham once he failed to attack, and might also lose some of those who had already joined him.

"Suppose we do have to defer our direct efforts," he wrote Owen, trying to encourage him, "shall great and noble minds . . . indulge in useless complaint. . . . Are our difficulties such as to make us give up one of the noblest enterprises in which men ever were engaged?"

He was back in Kansas by the end of June, but without any specific instructions. In fact, Gerrit Smith wrote Sanborn, "I do not wish to know Captain Brown's plans; I hope he will keep them to himself."

The month before Brown arrived, a band of Border Ruffians invaded a peaceful settlement called Trading Post. They took eleven free state settlers they found working in the fields, lined them up in a ravine near a marsh called the Swamp of the Swans, killed five, and wounded several others. One of the survivors was a blacksmith named Elias Snyder.

In early July, Brown (now using the name Shubel Morgan) and a handful of volunteers moved onto the Snyder farm, intending to protect the region from further attacks.

One of his new recruits was twenty-six-year-old Jeremiah G. Anderson, the great-grandson of a Revolutionary War soldier and a fierce opponent of slavery.

"Whose duty is it to help them [the slaves]?" he asked in a letter to his brother. "Is it yours, is it mine? It is every man's. . . ."

Shortly after moving onto the farm, Brown wrote Mary, "Deserted farms and dwellings lie in all directions for some miles along the line, and the remaining inhabitants watch every appearance of persons moving about with anxious vigilance."

Brown and his men waited at the farm for several weeks for word of trouble, but none came. Even while they waited, settlers flocked to the polls and rejected the proslavery constitution by a vote of 11,300 to 1,788. The struggle over slavery in Kansas was finally over.

One day while on reconnaissance with Snyder and Kagi just over the border in Missouri, Brown stopped on the crest of a hill that overlooked a cabin.

Suddenly Snyder said: "I declare that is Martin

White, reading a book in a chair in the shade of a tree. Suppose you and I go down and see the old man and have a talk with him."

Kagi was also eager to go and "have a talk" with the man who killed Frederick. To their surprise, however, Brown refused to give his permission.

"No, no, I can't do that," he said. "I would not hurt one hair on [White's] head. I would not go one inch to take his life; I do not harbour the feelings of revenge. *I act from a principle.* My aim and object is to restore human rights."

Brown then turned his horse and rode away.

During the months that followed he was often sick, and spent all of August in bed with fever. Kagi nursed him for four weeks before the fever finally broke and he was able to get out of bed.

"What course I shall next take, I cannot tell, till I have more strength," he wrote Mary in September of 1858.

Kansas continued to remain quiet throughout the fall and there was little for Brown to do. Then one day in December, that abruptly changed.

"As I was scouting down the line," said George Gill, one of Brown's volunteers, "I ran across a colored man."

His name was Jim Daniels and he said that he, his pregnant wife, their two children, and another man were going to be sold in a day or two by their Missouri slave owner. Daniels begged for help in escaping.

According to Gill, Brown saw this as an opportunity not only to strike at slave owners, but to prove the feasibility of his Virginia plan to the Secret Six.

The next day, he led a company of men — including several local volunteers — to the Missouri plantation where Daniels and his family lived. They rescued the five, then headed to a nearby plantation where they rescued five more people: a widow, her two grown daughters, one grown son, and a boy. A second group of volunteers rescued a woman named Jane from another slave owner.

The leader of the second group killed the slave owner after panicking over a sudden move by the man, but Brown made sure both slave owners he confronted were not harmed.

He then led the party back into Kansas.

It was the beginning of an escape odyssey as thrilling as any in the history of United States slavery: a one-thousand-one-hundred-mile, three-month journey toward Canada in the dead of winter through Kansas, Nebraska, Iowa, Illinois, and Michigan.

The governor of Missouri called the rescues a "dreadful outrage" and offered a reward of three thousand dollars for Brown's capture, while the governor of Kansas denounced the rescues as illegal acts against innocent people (the slave owners).

President Buchanan offered a reward of two hundred fifty dollars for Brown's capture, and United States cavalrymen — including Lieutenant J.E.B.

Stuart — rode out of Fort Leavenworth to track him down.

Brown sent the fugitives on ahead in a covered wagon, while he and his men stayed behind to fight off pursuers. At Osawatomie, the runaway men and women were hidden in an abandoned cabin for several days. Neighbors brought them food, and guarded the roads by night and day.

Brown resumed his journey with the fugitives, who now numbered twelve because Mrs. Daniels had given birth to "John Brown Daniels." Brown armed them with rifles, which they practiced with almost every day so they could defend themselves.

The fugitives were overjoyed to be free and, at first, said Samuel Harper, "we used to cut up all kinds of foolishness."

Then Brown would look at them "as solemn as a churchyard," but once in awhile he "let out de tiniest bit of a smile an' say: 'You'd better quit yo' foolin' . . .'"

Pursued by posses through bitter cold, over roads covered by snowdrifts, the lonely party found help from strangers.

Fifteen young white men from Topeka walked miles to find them and helped defeat a posse. When Brown and his supporters charged, members of the posse were so frantic to get away one "grabbed tight hold of the tail of a horse, trying to leap on from behind. . . . He went flying through the air, his feet touching the ground now and then."

Samuel Harper and his wife were freed, by Brown, from a plantation in Missouri.

Another time the fugitives were hiding in a house "when there came along a gang of slave-hunters," Harper said.

Brown wasn't there, but Aaron Stevens went out and had a long conversation with them, which worried Harper and the others.

"We began to get scared that Stevens was going to give us up to them slave hunters," Harper recalled. "But the looks of things changed when Stevens got up to the house. He just opened the door long enough for to grab a double-barreled gun. He pointed it at the slave hunter, and says: 'You want to see your slaves, does you? Well, just look up them barrels and see if you can find them.' That man went all to pieces. . . ."

Near the Nebraska border, Brown told a man about the fugitives "and asked if I could do anything to help them. . . . I went out among the houses and into several stores and got a number of pairs of shoes and some little money for the good cause."

When the man noticed the thinly-clad Brown trembling from the cold, he sat down, took off a pair of long johns he had purchased that day, and gave them to him.

Brown and his party were sheltered in Kansas by Native Americans and given food, clothing, and shelter by whites in many towns along the way. Residents throughout Iowa, Illinois, and Michigan seemed to welcome the opportunity to show their defiance of the Fugitive Slave Law and the slave posses that invaded their streets, even if many did not want black people living in their communities.

When the fugitives reached Chicago in March of 1859, they were hidden by black residents while Alan

Pinkerton, head of the famous detective agency, raised over five hundred dollars to send them on to Detroit in a boxcar.

The last Brown saw of them was when they boarded a ferry for Ontario and freedom. As they waited to leave, he said: "Lord, permit Thy servant to die in peace; for mine eyes have seen Thy salvation. I could not brook the thought that any ill should befall you [the slaves], least of all, that you should be taken back to slavery. The arm of Jehovah protected us."

That evening he met with Frederick Douglass and several black Detroit leaders, including George De-Baptiste, who once rescued a runaway by leading an attack on a courthouse. Brown apparently told of his plans to raid several Southern plantations, and gradually make the South "unsafe" for slavery.

DeBaptiste wasn't interested in taking years to make the South "unsafe" for slavery, and proposed instead that they start attacking slavery by blowing up fifteen large Southern white churches on a predetermined Sunday morning.

Brown seemed shocked by the proposal and said he did not want to shed blood unless it was absolutely necessary.

This meeting, like others Brown held with black leaders, produced little support for his plan. A large part of the reason may have been that people like DeBaptiste were used to carrying out bold actions in conjunction with other black people, and were reluctant to trust any white man when it came to the issue of slavery.

The next day, Brown sent eight of his men to Ashtabula, Ohio, where John, Jr., had hidden the guns, while he and Kagi traveled to Cleveland to try to raise money. They brought in a small amount from a lecture at Chapin's Hall, where they charged twenty-five cents for admission.

The city was in a tremendous state of excitement over the upcoming trial of thirty-seven black and white men for rescuing a fugitive slave from three deputy United States marshals. Two of the rescuers were Lewis Sheridan Leary and his nephew, John Copeland, who were being held with their companions in the Cleveland jail.

Residents from surrounding towns demonstrated outside the jail in support of the rescuers, and antislavery feeling ran high. There were posters throughout the city calling for Brown's arrest, but he walked defiantly by the marshal's office every day and was never bothered.

Brown even told a reporter that since President Buchanan had offered two hundred fifty dollars for his arrest, he was offering two dollars and fifty cents "for the safe delivery of the body of James Buchanan in any jail of the Free States."

After several days, Brown left Cleveland to visit

John, Jr., in Ashtabula. There he told his son to send the recruits from Kansas to a secret rendezvous in Virginia.

Kagi stayed in Cleveland to cover the trial of the rescuers for the *New York Tribune* and *Cleveland Leader,* and recruited two of them: Leary, who now lived in Oberlin with his wife, Mary, and their six-month-old child; and Copeland, a student at Oberlin College.

In April, 1859, Brown headed back East accompanied by Jeremiah Anderson. The trip was hard, with Brown once again falling ill with fever and "a terrible gathering" in his head.

He finally arrived at Peterboro, where he spoke so eloquently to Gerrit Smith and a small group of his friends that "Mr. Smith and some others wept."

Smith gave him several hundred dollars, with a promise of more to come. Brown then traveled to North Elba where he rested for several days and discussed his invasion plans with his family.

In early May, again trying to raise money, he lectured in Concord before an audience that included Emerson, Thoreau, Sanborn, and educator/philosopher Bronson Alcott (father of the writer, Louisa May Alcott).

That night Alcott wrote in his journal: "A young man named Anderson accompanies him. They go armed, I am told, and will defend themselves, if necessary. . . . The captain leaves us much in the dark concerning his destination and designs for the coming months. Yet . . . I think him equal to anything he dares — the man to do the deed, if it must be done. . . ."

Brown spent May 9, his fifty-ninth and last birthday, in Boston with Franklin Sanborn. The next day they met with Howe and Stearns to try to raise more money. Parker was in Europe trying to recuperate from a grave illness and Higginson refused to come, still angry that the plan had been postponed the previous year.

Brown was again sick, but talked enthusiastically to the rest of the Secret Six and a handful of other people. They contributed over two thousand dollars, with Stearns giving twelve hundred dollars of that amount.

Brown also attended a convention of the New England Antislavery Society, but grew so impatient listening to long speeches about overthrowing slavery, that he walked out in disgust.

"Talk! Talk! Talk!" he cried. "That will never free the slaves!"

He found time to send his family some badly needed supplies, as well as an inscribed Bible for five-year-old Ellen to remember him by. And then, the first week in June, he returned to North Elba for what would be his final visit to the mountains he loved so well.

He stayed just a little over a week, saying his good-byes to Mary, Ellen, and the rest of the family, and walking the fields for what he knew could be the last time.

Jason and Henry Thompson had already decided not to go South with him, and now Salmon joined them, saying "the trip was a mistake . . . it was not the wise thing to do."

Brown was bitterly disappointed and told Mary he regretted the decision as he "had never regretted the act of any of his children."

But Henry's brothers, William and Dauphin, promised to join him soon, and Watson said he would come, too, even though his wife, Isabel, had just given birth.

On the third week in June, Brown and Anderson rode away, heading for Ohio. There Brown gave John, Jr., instructions to try and raise more recruits and to ship the hidden weapons to Chambersburg, Pennsylvania, just forty-five miles north of Harpers Ferry.

Three months before Brown left North Elba for the South, newspapers told the nation about a huge sale of men, women, and children at a racetrack in Savannah, Georgia.

"The largest sale of human chattels that has been made in Star-Spangled America for several years took place on Wednesday and Thursday of last week," said a reporter in the *New York Daily Tribune*. ". . . The lot consisted of four-hundred and thirty-six men, women, children and infants . . ."

The sale lasted all week and brought in over three-hundred-thousand dollars. Thirty babies were among those sold, including one who was fifteen days old.

The baby's mother "was put up on the block with her husband and her other child, and with her new born baby in her arms, was sold to the highest bidder."

The reporter said babies "are esteemed worth to the master a hundred dollars the day they are born, and to increase in value at the rate of a hundred dollars a year till they are sixteen- or seventeen-years-old, at which age they bring the best prices."

A young couple who were engaged to be married were sold to separate owners and knew they would probably never see each other again. Jeffrey, "chattel No. 319," was sold to the owner of a rice plantation, and Dorcas, "chattel No. 278," was sold to the owner of a cotton plantation hundreds of miles away.

The last the reporter saw of them, Dorcas was "in the long room, sitting motionless as a statue, with her head covered with a shawl," and Jeffrey — trying to talk — "breaks down entirely and walks away, covering his face with his battered hat and sobbing like a very child."

In Troy, New York, Harriet Tubman helped storm a courthouse to free a fugitive named Charles Nalle.

When the men leading the assault were knocked down by policemen's clubs, said one observer, "Harriet and a number of other colored women rushed

Harriet Tubman gave Brown information about Southern escape routes.

over their bodies, brought Nalle out, and putting him in the first wagon passing, started him for the West."

Brown was counting on Harriet Tubman to raise recruits in Canada and to join his army herself.

In early July, 1859, Brown arrived in Harpers

Ferry, a town of about three thousand, hemmed in by water and cliffs hundreds of feet high. It was located where the Shenandoah and Potomac rivers collided "in quest of a passage," as Thomas Jefferson had written more than seventy years before Brown's arrival. "In the moment of their junction they rush together against the mountain, rend it asunder, and pass off to the sea."

On a narrow strip of land, built to take advantage of the water power, stood the United States arsenal, armory, and engine house. On a nearby island was Hall's Rifle Works, where sixty expert gunsmiths made ten thousand weapons a year for the United States Army.

Calling himself Isaac Smith, a farmer and cattle buyer from New York, Brown quietly rented the Kennedy farm on the Maryland side of the Potomac, a few miles northeast of Harpers Ferry. Only Owen, Oliver, and Jeremiah Anderson were with him.

Others would come in the weeks ahead. In the meantime, Brown continued to make plans and to study the maps and papers he brought with him, including the Chatham Declaration of Independence.

And now, as he began to make his final preparations to attack slavery, perhaps he felt more intensely than ever the words he had expressed months before in the Declaration's final two lines:

"Nature is morning [sic] for its murdered, and Afflicted Children. Hung be the Heavens in Scarlet!"

■

CHAPTER EIGHT

GET ON YOUR ARMS

Now that he was finally ready to strike at the heart of slavery, Brown was once again delayed by an old problem: a shortage of money. He was even forced to urge Watson and Dauphin not to come until they made arrangements to feed the family livestock throughout the winter.

"I write to say . . . that I think Watson and D. had not best set out until we write again," he told Mary in a letter three weeks after moving onto the Kennedy farm, "and not until sufficient hay has been secured to winter all the stock well. To be buying hay in the spring or last of the winter is ruinous. . . ."

In the meantime, Brown sent for fifteen-year-old Annie and seventeen-year-old Martha Evelyn (Oliver's wife) to come and divert suspicion from the all-male household.

Martha did the cooking and helped the men with the housework, while Annie served as chief "outside guard" — sitting on the porch and watching for neighbors who dropped by unexpectedly.

Brown asked Sanborn to raise more money from the Secret Six, and to find Harriet Tubman so she could participate in the attack.

"I conclude that your operations will not be delayed if the money reaches you in course of the next fortnight, . . ." Sanborn replied. "I cannot certainly promise that you will [have it then], but I think so. Harriet Tubman is probably in New Bedford, sick."

John Kagi, now using the name "John Henrie," stayed at a boarding house run by an antislavery woman in Chambersburg. There, with the help of a black barber and Underground Railroad conductor named Henry Watson, he made arrangements to forward the mail, recruits, and "hardware" [weapons] John, Jr., was preparing to send.

Brown was so concerned about money, however, he told Kagi that if Leary and Copeland were not already on their way to the Kennedy farm, "have them wait till we are better prepared. . . . Do not send or bring any more persons here until we advise you of our readiness to board them."

By the first week in August, however, several of the men were there: Watson, the Thompson brothers, Aaron Stevens, Edwin and Barclay Coppoc, and Charles Tidd.

The Kennedy farm, where John Brown gathered his group for the attack on Harpers Ferry.

Most of the weapons arrived by freight in Chambersburg, "but the bills are very high," Brown wrote John, Jr., "and I begin to be apprehensive of getting into a tight spot for want of a little more funds, notwithstanding my anxiety to make my money hold out. . . . All my accounts are squared up to the present time; but how I can keep my little wheels in motion for a few days more I am beginning to feel at a loss. . . . Our hands so far are coming forward promptly, and better than I expected, as we have called on them. We have to move with all caution."

Brown often conferred with Kagi in Chambersburg, traveling there "sometimes on old Dolly, his brown mule, and sometimes in the wagon."

At the farm, he spent hours every day writing letters asking for support, or preparing "General Orders No. 1," which detailed the organizational structure of his Provisional Army.

One morning while he was writing and Annie was sewing, two birds kept flying in through the door, then back out to their nest, "fluttering and twittering." Annie was troubled by their behavior, so she and her father went outside to investigate.

A snake "was just ready to devour the little ones in the nest," Annie said. "Father killed the snake; and then the old birds sat on the railing and sang as if they would burst. . . . After we went back into the room, he said he thought it very strange the way the birds asked him to help them, and asked if I thought it an omen of success. He seemed very much impressed with that idea."

Brown wanted Frederick Douglass to join in the attack on Harpers Ferry, so he arranged a secret rendezvous at an old stone quarry in Chambersburg. Kagi accompanied Brown, who was disguised as a fisherman, and Shields Green came with Douglass. The four sat down among the rocks and, for the first time, Brown told Douglass he was going to attack the arsenal at Harpers Ferry.

The attack, he declared, "would serve as notice to the slaves that their friends had come, and as a trumpet to rally them to his standard."

"I at once opposed it with all the arguments at my command," Douglass said. "To me, such a measure would be fatal to running off slaves [the original plan], and fatal to all engaged. It would be an attack on the Federal Government, and would array the whole country against us. . . . I told him . . . that he was going into a perfect steel-trap, and that once in, he would not get out alive. . . ."

Brown replied that he would be able to dictate terms for safe passage out of town, because he would have hostages.

"I told him that Virginia would blow him and his hostages sky-high rather than that he should hold Harpers Ferry an hour," Douglass said. "Our talk was long and earnest. . . ."

They argued all that day and part of the next, but neither would budge.

Finally, Douglass stood up to leave and Brown made one last effort to convince him.

"Come with me, Douglass," he said, embracing him. "I will defend you with my life. I want you for a special purpose. When I strike, the bees will begin to swarm, and I shall want you to help hive them."

But, refusing once again, Douglass turned to Green and asked "what he had decided to do, and was surprised by his saying, in his broken way, 'I b'lieve I'll go wid de ole man.'"

And so a disappointed Brown returned to the farm without the man he knew the slaves would trust and follow, more than they would trust and follow any white man. But he had gained a new black recruit, though he almost lost him a few days later.

While Owen was guiding Shields Green to the farm, they suddenly found themselves chased into a wood by slave catchers. When their pursuers went back for reinforcements, Owen "took Green on his back and swam across the river."

A few days later, Douglass received a letter signed by several black men in Philadelphia. Referring in guarded words to the attack on Harpers Ferry, they urged that "our class (black people) be properly represented in a convention to come off right away [near] Chambersburg. . . ."

If Douglass would go, they said, "Some of our members are ready to go with you," but Douglass refused to reconsider.

At almost the same time Brown was meeting with Douglass, Dangerfield Newby received another anguished plea from his wife.

"It is said Master is in want of money," she wrote. "If so, I know not what time he may sell me, *an* then all my bright *hope* of the *futer* are blasted . . . for if I thought I *shoul* never see you this earth would have no charms for me. Do all you can for me, *witch* I have no doubt you will. . . ."

Soon after receiving this letter, the forty-four-year-old Newby joined Brown's men at the farm.

As their numbers grew, it became more and more difficult to hide them from prying neighbors. The men were confined to the house during the day and often had to rush to the attic when visitors suddenly showed up.

Most of his neighbors seemed to think of Brown as a friendly farmer who was, as one said later, "a good neighbor, and a good preacher, too. He preached in the little church by the roadside."

But one woman who was always making surprise visits, walked into the house one day before anyone could stop her and spotted Shields Green before he could hide.

"She thought these strangers were running off negroes to the North," Annie said. "I used to give her everything she wanted or asked for to keep her on good terms, but we were in constant fear that she was either a spy or would betray us. It was like standing on a powder magazine, after a slow match had been lighted."

Now that Douglass had turned him down, Brown was more anxious than ever for Harriet Tubman to join him. He asked John, Jr., and Sanborn to find her, but she apparently had fallen ill somewhere in New England.

Annie Brown, daughter of John Brown.

When Brown revealed his plan to all his followers, some responded with a near mutiny. They had come to help run off slaves as Brown had done in the Missouri raid, not to attack a United States arsenal.

Tidd was so angry he left the farm for a week, staying with Cook at his house in Harpers Ferry. Kagi supported the raid, arguing that if they took Harpers Ferry by surprise, they could quickly move into the mountains and set up their mountain state.

Cook also "favored the capture quite forcibly."

But Brown's own sons voiced strong opposition, saying it would be suicidal for a handful of men to try to hold the town against state militia and federal troops. Oliver had made several trips to Harpers Ferry, and said they could easily be trapped because of the surrounding rivers and mountains.

The discussion went on for hours, and finally Oliver — speaking for himself, Owen, and Watson — said they would follow him wherever he led.

"We must not let our father die alone," Oliver declared.

Shields Green and Dangerfield Newby had supported Brown all along, and now everyone joined in.

Soon afterward, on a trip in the wagon from the farm to Chambersburg, Brown told Owen, "I feel so depressed on account of the opposition of the men, that at times I am almost willing to temporarily abandon the undertaking."

"We have gone too far for that," Owen replied, "we must go ahead."

When they returned to the farm, Brown resigned and told the men to choose another leader, but they quickly reelected him.

"We have all agreed to sustain your decisions, until you have *proved* incompetent," Owen said, "and many of us will adhere to your decisions so long as you will."

There were now eighteen recruits. They spent much of their time studying a manual of military tactics, singing, debating, and reading everything from Thomas Paine's *Age of Reason* to the newspapers and magazines Kagi sent down from Chambersburg.

One day when there was a thunderstorm and they were certain no one could hear, they raced up and down the stairs yelling and screaming like wild men, trying to rid themselves of the pressure of confinement.

Hazlett and Leeman even crept out at night to go for walks in the woods, or into Harpers Ferry to visit Cook.

The men also wrote so many letters divulging details of the raid that an angry Brown told Kagi, "If every one must write some *girl*; or some other *extra* friend, telling or shoing [sic] our location; and telling *(as some have done)* all about our matters; we might as well get the whole published at *once*, in the *New York Herald*. Any person is a *stupid fool* who expects his *friends* to keep *for him*; that which he cannot keep himself. . . ."

The pressures grew on the men, however, and several became convinced their secret had been discovered and a mob would descend at any moment and kill them all. But still they stayed, more convinced than ever of the evils of slavery and more determined than ever to end it.

"We have only two black men with us now," Watson wrote his wife, Isabel, "[and] one of these has a wife and seven children in slavery. I sometimes feel as though I could not make the sacrifice, but what would I want others to do were I in their place?"

Later, Watson told her about the suicide of a slave "near here whose wife was sold off South the other day. . . . Cannot come home so long as such things are done here. . . . There was another murder committed near our place the other day, making in all five murders and one suicide within five miles . . . they were all slaves, too. . . ."

There were relatively few slaves in the Harpers Ferry area, but because of incidents like these, they were said to be in an angry mood.

In the midst of preparing for the attack on the arsenal, Brown found time to respond to a letter from Mary: "I do not know what to advise about fattening the old spotted cow, as much will depend on what you have to feed her with . . . I know but little about your crops. I should like to know more as soon as I can. . . ."

Still trying to raise more money and recruits, he made a hurried trip to Philadelphia to meet with several black supporters. They gave him a little money, but no recruits, and he returned to the farm with an "overflowing, saddened heart. . . ."

One day the men sat down and counted their money. Brown was shocked to find the total was less than five dollars, and he considered calling off the attack.

All his life he had shown an amazing strength —

Daguerreotype of John Brown.

or weakness — to delay plans until he felt the time was right. Now he was delaying again.

Before Watson left North Elba, Salmon had said, "You know father . . . [he] would insist on getting everything arranged just to suit him before he would consent to make a move."

Such a delay, Salmon predicted, might result in all of them being captured or killed.

But Brown felt he could not move without money to supply his men once they made it to the mountains, and so he waited for a sign, such as the one given him when the two birds "asked" for his help.

A friend in Chatham wrote that Osborne Anderson was on his way, and added: "More laborers may be looked for shortly."

One night near the end of September, Brown drove his wagon to the Maryland border and picked up Anderson.

"We set out directly," the young printer said, "and drove until nearly day-break . . . when we reached the Farm in safety. As a very necessary precaution against surprise, all the colored men at the Ferry who went from the North, made the journey from the Pennsylvania line in the night."

Anderson was greeted warmly by the others, and found them all totally committed to helping "the suffering and pleading slave. . . . In John Brown's house, and in John Brown's presence, men from widely different parts of the continent met and united into one company . . . no ghost of a distinction found space to enter."

Anderson said that every morning Brown gathered "the family" together, read the Bible to them, and prayed aloud.

"I never heard John Brown pray," Anderson said, "that he did not make strong appeals to God for the deliverance of the slave."

At the end of September, Brown sent Annie and Martha home. The night before they left, Shields Green gave a farewell speech, "as he called it," Annie said. "This was the greatest conglomeration of big words that was ever piled up. Some one asked Anderson 'if he understood it,' and he replied, 'No, God Himself could not understand that.'"

The arrival of Anderson and the promise of more recruits to come must have lifted Brown's spirits, and he now said he planned to "move about the end of the month."

But money was still a problem. Kagi wrote friends in Boston that "Captain Brown's men were in need of more money and could not begin their movements until it reached them."

Black abolitionist and Underground Railroad conductor Lewis Hayden heard of the letter and asked Francis Jackson Meriam, the twenty-one-year-old son of a prominent abolitionist, to give him five hundred dollars. Meriam had traveled to Kansas two years before to join Brown's forces, but was unable to find him.

Hearing that Brown was about to lead an attack in Virginia, he told Hayden "you can have my money and me along with it."

Meriam made out his will, leaving most of his property to the Massachusetts Abolition Society, then traveled south. He reached the farm on October 15, just a few hours after Lewis Leary and John Copeland arrived. Several other recruits were reportedly on their way, but Kagi had already taken steps to stop them.

"You must by all means keep back the men you talked of sending until you receive further instructions," he wrote John, Jr., a few days before the last recruits arrived. ". . . We must first make a complete and indisputably open road to the free states. That will require both labor and time. . . ."

Then suddenly, after delaying so long, Brown decided to attack the following evening — barely thirty-six hours away.

Neighbors had noticed an unusual number of "express packages" were being delivered to the farm. And one day during the past week, several of the men had grown so weary of being cooped up they went out in the daytime.

"Not being fully satisfied as to the real business of 'J. Smith & Sons' after that, . . ." Anderson said, "threats to search the premises were made against the encampment. . . . Captain Brown . . . concluded to strike the blow immediately. . . ."

Brown had also been told the government was about to transfer several thousand rifles from Harpers Ferry to other arsenals in the South, to be used against the North in case of war, and that may have played a part in his decision.

All day Saturday the men worked feverishly, preparing to move supplies to a schoolhouse Brown had chosen as a rendezvous point after the attack. The next day, a Sunday, he rose earlier than usual and called the men to worship.

"He read a chapter from the Bible," Anderson recalled, "applicable to the condition of the slave, and our duty as their brethren, and then offered up a fervent prayer to God to assist in the liberation of the bondmen in that slaveholding land."

Next, Brown called for a council of war, and appointed Osborne Anderson to preside. Battle assignments and army commissions were handed out by Brown, acting as commander-in-chief. Each of the black men was offered a commission, but all declined because, said Anderson, of "a want of acquaintance with military tactics."

In the afternoon, Brown read eleven orders aloud, detailing the plan of attack and the sequence for it to be carried out. George Washington's nephew, Colonel Lewis Washington, owned slaves at a nearby plantation, and possessed a sword given to George Washington by Frederick the Great, and a pistol given him by Lafayette.

Brown's last order called for Colonel Washington, who was also an aide to the governor of Virginia, to be taken prisoner and deliver the sword and pistol "into the hands of Osborne P. Anderson. Anderson being a colored man, and colored men being only *things* in the South, it is proper that the South be taught a lesson upon this point."

After Brown finished reading the orders, the men spent the rest of the day quietly, alone with their thoughts. There were twenty-one of them, five black and sixteen white. Most were in their twenties, while Dangerfield Newby, the oldest, was forty-four.

Thirteen of the recruits had fought against slavery in Kansas, and some, like Watson and Oliver, had only recently married.

"Oh, Bell," Watson wrote in one of his last letters, "I do want to see you and the little fellow very much, but I must wait. . . ."

In a letter she would not receive until after his death, Oliver told Martha, "You can hardly think how I want to see you, or how lonesome it was the day I left you. . . . Nothing else could strengthen me to do the right thing so much as the thought of you. . . ."

And in his last letter to his mother, twenty-year-

Oliver Brown and his wife, Martha Brewster Brown.

old William Leeman — the youngest member of the group — said: "Yes, mother, I am warring with slavery, the greatest curse that ever infested America. . . . I am in a good cause and I am not afraid. I know my mother will not object. You have a generous heart. I know you will sacrifice something for your fellow beings in bondage. . . ."

In Oberlin, Lewis Leary used to listen to fugitives tell of their experiences in slavery, "signifying often by the deep scowl of his countenance, the moist condition of his eyes and the quivering of his lips, how deeply he was moved by the recital of wrong and outrage," a friend remembered.

Now Leary, who left his wife of a year without telling her where he was going or what he planned to do, waited for nightfall. His thoughts must have been on the woman he loved and the six-month-old baby he would never see again.

And so the twenty-one men passed their final hours at the farm.

"Be cheerful," Kagi had written his father and sister a few weeks before. "Don't imagine dangers. All will be well."

Brown carefully placed several papers in a carpetbag, including letters from Sanborn, Smith, Douglass, and others, and maps of seven Southern states with slave population statistics written in the margins. He then stored the carpetbag in a trunk on the first floor of the farmhouse.

Brown often told his children while they were growing up that, "One man and God can change the universe." Now he was ready to act on that belief and try to change, not the universe, but the country and its practice of slavery.

When nightfall came, he gathered the men about him and said: "And now, gentlemen, let me impress this one thing upon your minds. You all know how dear life is to you, and how dear life is to your friends. And in remembering that, consider that the lives of others are as dear to them as yours are to you.

Do not, therefore, take the life of any one, if you can possibly avoid it; but if it is necessary to take life in order to save your own, then make sure work of it."

At eight o'clock he told them: "Men, get on your arms; we will proceed to the Ferry."

They walked outside where Meriam, Owen Brown, and Barclay Coppoc, who were assigned to guard the farmhouse, exchanged good-byes. Then Brown "put on his old Kansas cap, and gave the final order at Kennedy farm: 'Come, boys!'"

He drove his creaking wagon, now loaded with pikes, a crowbar, and a sledgehammer, down the hill to the main road. The men, wrapped in long gray shawls to guard against the cold and a slight rain, followed in pairs.

They proceeded with "some distance" between each pair, as Brown had ordered, so that anyone they met could be detained by two of them "until the rest of our comrades were out of the road."

Cook and Tidd, the ones most familiar with the surrounding countryside, led the way so they could cut the telegraph lines leading into and out of town.

And so the tiny Provisional Army left the farm, walking through the night toward Harpers Ferry "as silently as a funeral procession," said Osborne Anderson.

It was almost ten o'clock when the men followed Brown into the covered wagon and railroad bridge that led across the Potomac River into Harpers Ferry.

Brown ordered them to halt and fasten their cartridge belts outside their clothes, so the forty cartridges each carried would be easier to reach once the fighting began.

Then finally, said Anderson, "everything was ready for the taking of the town."

CHAPTER NINE

A BROKEN-WINGED HAWK

Kagi and Stevens dashed onto the Potomac bridge and took the watchman prisoner. Brown then drove onto the bridge in his wagon, ordering Watson and Stewart Taylor to remain behind as guards while he and the others proceeded to the armory.

They were now in Virginia, the birthplace of slavery in the United States.

They found the gates to the armory yard locked, said Anderson, "and the watchman on the inside. He was told to open the gates, but refused . . . The men were then ordered by Captain Brown to open the gates forcibly, which was done, and the watchman taken prisoner."

Brown, Edwin Coppoc, and Albert Hazlett stood guard at the armory while the remaining fourteen rushed to their assignments in different parts of town.

About this time, said Anderson, "there was apparently much excitement. People were passing back and forth in the town, and before we could do much, we had to take several prisoners."

Once the prisoners were secured, Brown ordered Hazlett and Coppoc to capture and guard the nearby arsenal, which they quickly did. Kagi and John Copeland took control of the rifle works a half mile away, while Oliver Brown and William Thompson seized the Shenandoah wagon bridge, about three hundred yards from the covered bridge.

A view of Harpers Ferry; covered bridge is at lower left.

By midnight, just two hours after they entered Harpers Ferry, Brown and his men had captured the armory, arsenal, rifle works, and two bridges "without the snap of a gun, or any violence whatever," said Anderson.

Brown then sent a party commanded by Aaron Stevens into the countryside to take prisoners, including Colonel Washington, and bring back any slaves willing to come. Besides Cook and Tidd, the group included three of the army's black members: Anderson, Shields Green, and Lewis Leary.

"On the road we met some colored men, to whom we made known our purpose, when they immediately agreed to join us," Anderson declared. "They said they had been long waiting for an opportunity of the kind. . . . The result was that many colored men gathered to the scene of action."

Leary and Green guarded the approach to Washington's house, while the others went inside. Washington was nowhere to be seen, but finally opened a bedroom door and begged them not to kill him. He said they could take his slaves if they would leave him alone.

"No," Stevens replied, "you must go along too; so get ready."

"The colonel cried heartily when he found he must submit," Anderson said, "and appeared taken aback when, on delivering up the famous sword presented to his illustrious kinsman, George Washington, Captain Stevens told me to step forward and take it."

The party started back to Harpers Ferry in Washington's large, four-horse wagon, stopping at the plantation of a nearby slave owner named John Allstadt. Like Washington, he offered to surrender his slaves if they would leave him alone, but Stevens also took him and his son prisoner.

Several of the slaves came with the group, said Anderson, "by their own consent. . . ."

It was almost three A.M. when the party stopped at the home of an elderly black woman, who "had a good time over the message we took her," Anderson recalled. "This liberating the slaves was the very thing she had longed for, prayed for, and dreamed about. . . ."

But slowly, and almost without Brown's knowing it, the tide began to turn against him and his men.

At about one-thirty A.M., the eastbound train from Wheeling was halted by Brown's men. Hearing the commotion, the porter/ticket agent — a free black man named Hayward Shepherd — walked out to the bridge to see what was happening.

"Halt!" one of the raiders cried.

Shepherd turned and started running, and either Watson or Stewart Taylor fired at him, the shots taking "effect in his back, going through his body and coming out at the nipple of his left breast."

Shepherd was pulled into the railroad office, where he died several hours later. Ironically, the first fatality in Brown's attempt to free black people was a free black man.

By now the townspeople were aroused. The shot and the commotion around the armory and in the streets quickly fed rumors of a massive slave revolt: the long-feared white Southern nightmare that another Nat Turner had come.

The bell of the Lutheran church tolled wildly, calling out to people in town and country: *slave rebellion!*

Two men leaped onto their horses and raced toward other communities, yelling "insurrection!" as they went, and soon bells were pealing through the night in other towns: Charlestown, Martinsburg, and Shepherdstown.

The volunteer militia organizations, whose primary purpose was to control slaves, began to mobilize and to head to Harpers Ferry. But in the town itself, Brown quietly talked to his prisoners as if he had all the time in the world.

"You will find a fire in here, sir," he told Washington when he arrived. "It is rather cool this morning."

"I shall be very attentive to you, sir," he said a little later, "for I may get the worst of it in my first encounter, and if so, your life is worth as much as mine. . . . I wanted you particularly for the moral effect it would give our cause having one of your name as a prisoner. . . ."

Several townspeople who ventured out were also taken prisoner, including a bartender at the hotel next to the armory.

At five A.M., Brown sent Cook, Tidd, Leeman, and at least four of the liberated slaves — now armed — to the Kennedy farm to help move the weapons and supplies to the schoolhouse. The group left in Colonel Washington's wagon, further splintering the little army.

Brown would retain control of Harpers Ferry for several more hours, but he seemed to have forgotten the advice he gave the black Gileadites almost twenty years before: "get the job disposed of before the number that an uproar would bring together can collect."

At dawn on Monday, in a move that must have puzzled his followers, he decided to let the passenger train proceed, walking across the bridge with the conductor "with cool deliberation and as much unconcern as if carrying on an ordinary business proceeding. . . . [Then] he waited . . . till the signal to proceed was given, and then walked back over it alone."

According to the train engineer, a man named William Wooley, dozens of slaves had gathered around the cars of the stopped train, shouting that they wanted their freedom.

In letting the train proceed, it was as if Brown wanted the world to know what he was doing, even if the knowledge caused his defeat. And the world soon knew because the passengers, "taking all the paper they could find, wrote accounts of the insurrection, which they threw from the windows as the train rushed onward."

Word spread by telegraph from New York to San Francisco, and the nation's newspapers soon reflected the fear felt by the white residents of Harpers Ferry:

"EXTENSIVE SLAVE CONSPIRACY IN MARYLAND AND VIRGINIA!"

"HUNDREDS OF INSURRECTIONISTS IN ARMS!"

"NEGRO INSURRECTION AT HARPERS FERRY!!"

Brown ordered Osborne Anderson to pass out pikes to "the colored men who had come with us from the plantations, and others who had come forward without having had communication with any of our party."

By this time it was daylight, and men, women, and children could be seen "leaving their homes in all directions," said Anderson, "climbing up the hillsides, evidently impelled by a sudden fear, which was plainly visible in their countenances or in their movements. Captain Brown was all activity, though at times he appeared somewhat puzzled."

Brown sent Lewis Leary to join Kagi, Copeland, and three slaves at the rifle works, and when Leeman returned from the farm, he was ordered there, too.

OLIVER BROWN

OWEN BROWN

WATSON BROWN

DAUPHIN THOMPSON

EDWIN COPPOC

SHIELDS GREEN

STEWART TAYLOR

CHARLES E. TIDD

OSBORNE ANDERSON

Pictured on these pages are some of the men who followed John Brown in the raid at Harpers Ferry.

WILLIAM H. LEEMAN

JOHN E. COOK

JOHN H. COPELAND

AARON D. STEVENS

ALBERT HAZLETT

BARCLAY COPPOC

JEREMIAH ANDERSON

DANGERFIELD NEWBY

LEWIS LEARY

In the middle of all this activity, Brown took time out to order breakfast for his men and the prisoners from the local hotel, freeing the bartender in exchange for the meals.

He also spent valuable time trying to convince his prisoners that slavery was immoral.

"During the day and night I talked much with Brown," said a prisoner named John Daingerfield. "I found him as brave as a man could be, and sensible upon all subjects except slavery. Upon that question he was a religious fanatic, and believed it was his duty to free the slaves, even if in so doing he lost his own life."

Throughout the early morning hours, farmers and other men from the surrounding countryside arrived and "broke into liquor saloons, filled up, and . . . kept shouting, shooting at random, and howling."

When a man shot at Coppoc, who was guarding the armory gate, an elderly slave who had joined Brown's men promptly fired a load of buckshot at the attacker, who "fell, and expired without a struggle." The gun the slave used belonged to Colonel Washington.

Several citizens began to shoot at Kagi's position and he sent urgent messages to Brown urging that the scattered force be consolidated and withdrawn from town. Stevens and others also urged Brown to withdraw, but he continued to hold fast.

Owen and the others assigned to transfer the

weapons and supplies to the schoolhouse had still not returned. Their task, which should have taken about four hours, took ten. Cook even stopped the work for several minutes to lecture a slave owner about the immorality of slavery.

At about noon on Monday, the Jefferson Guards militia arrived from Charlestown and prepared to storm the covered bridge. Brown hurried into the street with Frederick the Great's sword on his hip, calling for his men to follow. Dangerfield Newby, Dauphin Thompson, Aaron Stevens, Osborne Anderson, and several of the liberated slaves raced to join him.

"The troops are on the bridge coming into town; we will give them a warm reception," Anderson remembered Brown saying "as he walked among us, giving words of encouragement. . . .

"The troops soon came out of the bridge and up the street facing us . . . When they got within sixty or seventy yards, Captain Brown said: 'Let go upon them!'

"Which we did, when several of them fell. Again and again was the fire repeated. . . . The consequence of their unexpected reception was after leaving several of their dead on the field, the Marylanders beat a confused retreat into the bridge. . . ."

Two of the slaves were killed in the fighting, but none of Brown's other men were hurt until they started back to the armory. Suddenly a shot rang out from the window of a store and Newby fell face downward.

He managed to shoot back, but a second shot rang out and an iron slug cut his throat from ear to ear. Shields Green fired and killed the assailant before he could get his gun out of the window.

In Newby's pocket when he died was the last letter from Harriet, pleading for him to "*Com* as soon as you can . . . Oh, that *bless* hour when I shall see you once more. . . ."

Now the Potomac bridge was in the hands of the militia, and soon they would also seize the Shenandoah bridge and the houses across from the arsenal.

"As more and more men poured into the town," said Anderson, "the enemy took positions round about, so as to prevent any escape, within shooting distance of the engine-house and arsenal.

Captain Brown, seeing their maneuvers, said, 'We will hold on to our three positions, if they are unwilling to come to terms, and die like men.'"

Kagi sent word that his ammunition was running low, he could not hold out much longer, and the army should retreat before it was too late.

"The message sent back to Kagi was to hold out for a few minutes longer, when we would all evacuate the place," said Anderson. "Those few minutes proved disastrous. . . ."

Later Brown would say: "I should have gone away;

but I had thirty-odd prisoners, whose wives and daughters were in tears for their safety, and I felt for them. Besides, I wanted to allay the fears of those who believed we came here to burn and kill. For this reason I allowed the train to cross the bridge. . . ."

Brown and his men were now being fired on by hundreds of men, with more militia companies arriving.

President Buchanan, receiving a report that "seven hundred whites and Negroes" were in the invasion force, ordered three artillery companies and ninety Marines to Harpers Ferry.

The scattered forces of the Provisional Army were totally isolated from each other: Brown, taking the most important prisoners with him, retreated first into the armory grounds and then into the fortresslike fire engine house, where he "began at once to bar the doors and windows, and to cut port holes through the brick wall."

Kagi, Copeland, and Leary faced a withering fire at the rifle works; Hazlett and Osborne Anderson held out in the arsenal; and Cook, Tidd, and the others were still moving supplies to the schoolhouse outside of town.

In mid-afternoon a large force attacked the rifle works, and Kagi, Leary, Copeland, and two of the slaves who had joined them were driven into the Shenandoah. Kagi was the first to die, his body riddled with bullets. Thirty miles to the south, the waters of the Shenandoah flowed through the lands of his father's family.

The two slaves were the next to die, and then Leary was wounded by several shots while trying to swim the river.

He was carried to a workshop where several reporters interviewed him. Leary begged them to tell his wife what had happened and then, after suffering for ten more hours, he died. At least one resident clubbed his lifeless body.

Copeland reached a large rock in the middle of the river and turned to face his pursuer, a Harpers Ferry resident named James Holt.

Both their weapons had been rendered useless by the water, but Holt, "as he . . . advanced, continued to snap his gun, while Copeland did the same."

The crowd on the shore screamed, "Lynch him! Lynch the nigger!" when Copeland was taken prisoner.

They started tying a noose to hang him when a local doctor shielded Copeland and kept him safe until he could be taken away by the militia.

Thousands of shots now rained into the engine house, shattering every window, penetrating the walls, and blowing holes in the doors almost big enough for a man to crawl through.

Throughout the firing, said John Daingerfield, "when his men would want to fire upon some one who might be seen passing, Brown would stop them, saying, 'Don't shoot; that man is unarmed.'"

Watching the arrival of hundreds of militiamen, Hazlett and Anderson decided to escape from the arsenal while they could. Shortly after they made this decision, Shields Green came running under fire with a message from Brown. Anderson told him their plan and urged him to leave with them.

Green was silent at first, then looked back at the engine house and said, "You think der's no chance, Osborne?"

"Not one," Anderson replied.

"And the old Captain can't get away?"

"No," Anderson and Hazlett both replied.

"Well," said Green with a long and slow utterance, "I guess I'll go back to de old man."

Looking back on this scene years later, Anderson said: "Wiser and better men no doubt there were, but a braver man never lived than Shields Green."

Drunken crowds now swarmed through the streets, shooting wildly in the air. A company of militia from Martinsburg rushed through the armory yard from the rear, freeing several prisoners and cutting off Brown's last escape route. The jaws of the "perfect steel trap" had now clanged shut.

Brown sent William Thompson out to negotiate safe passage in exchange for the release of the prisoners.

Thompson carried a flag of truce, but was immediately seized and taken to the hotel as a prisoner. A mob led by Harry Hunter, son of Virginia's special attorney, burst into the room and dragged Thompson out by the throat.

"You may take my life," Thompson cried, [but] "eighty thousand will arise to avenge me, and carry out my purpose of giving liberty to the slaves."

They shot him in the head and flung his body into the water near the covered bridge. For the rest of the afternoon the townspeople used his body for target practice.

Earlier, young Leeman was shot to death by a militiaman while trying to escape. "Don't shoot," Leeman had shouted, raising his hands. But the man fired at him point-blank, blowing the youth's face into a bloody pulp while the crowd cheered.

The body of Newby was dragged into a gutter by a cursing crowd, his ears cut off for souvenirs, sticks shoved into his wounds and his body beaten over and over again.

The howling mob, said a reporter, "wished he had a thousand lives wherewith to appease their fury."

In late afternoon, Brown again tried to negotiate, sending Watson out under a flag of truce. As soon as he appeared outside, however, he was gunned down. Watson managed to crawl back into the engine house, where he fought for another hour and a half before being wounded again. This time he doubled up in great agony at his father's feet, moaning in pain.

At the urging of the prisoners, who were afraid of being killed in all the shooting, Brown then sent Stevens out under a flag of truce. The mob promptly fired at Stevens, however, and he lay bleeding in the gutter until a prisoner volunteered to carry him inside the railroad station.

There were now about a thousand men firing on the engine house, but Brown and his men continued to hold them off with "volley after volley" that mingled with "the echoes from the hills, the shrieks of the townspeople, and the groans of their wounded and dying, all of which filled the air. . . ."

John Brown and his men inside the engine house.

Militiamen raced into the arsenal, but Anderson and Copeland had already escaped, crossing the Potomac in a boat and fleeing through the hills toward the Kennedy farm.

In the arsenal, Stewart Taylor lay dead and Oliver Brown was dying on the floor beside Watson, both groaning in their agony. Edwin Coppoc, who had been wounded, peered through a gunhole and realized Cook was firing on their attackers from the heights overlooking the town.

"There were thirty or forty men in the first party he fired on who after the second shot were taken with a sudden leaving," Coppoc said, "having no doubt important business elsewhere."

Cook fired a few shots, then hurried to the schoolhouse where Owen, Barclay Coppoc, Tidd, and Meriam were anxiously waiting to find out how the fight was going.

When nightfall came, the inside of the engine house grew dark and cold.

"It had rained some little all day and the atmosphere was raw and cold," said one townsman. "Now, a cloudy and moonless sky hung like a pall over the scene of war, and, on the whole, a more dismal night cannot be imagined."

In Charlestown, a mob took out their anger at Brown and his men by breaking into the jail, dragging out a black prisoner and lynching him.

Now, only four of Brown's men were unhurt: Shields Green, Edwin Coppoc, Jeremiah Anderson, and Dauphin Thompson.

Brown, still wearing George Washington's sword (which he had promised to return to Colonel Washington), paced back and forth. Occasionally he called out, "Men, are you awake?"

Oliver was in such agony, said one prisoner, he begged his father "again and again to be shot," but Brown answered: "If you must die, die like a man."

After awhile he called out to Oliver and there was no answer.

He walked over to Oliver, straightened out his limbs and said, "This is the third son I have lost in this cause."

At about midnight the marines arrived, commanded by Colonel Robert E. Lee, who sent Lieutenant J.E.B. Stuart with a note demanding unconditional surrender.

When Brown rejected the terms, declaring that surrender would mean death for him and his men, Stuart said he would return in the morning for a final reply. Brown and his men immediately began barricading the doors and windows, preparing for the attack they knew would come at dawn.

"During all this time," said Captain Daingerfield, "not one of Brown's men showed the slightest fear, but calmly awaited the attack, selecting the best situations to fire from upon the attacking party, and arranging their guns and pistols so that a fresh one could be taken up as soon as one was discharged. . . ."

Throughout the night Brown treated his prisoners with courtesy, said Daingerfield, even though his sons had been "shot down beside him, [and] almost any other man similarly placed would at least have exacted life for life."

At one point Brown told his prisoners: "Gentlemen, if you knew of my past history you would not blame me for being here. I went to Kansas a peaceable man, and the proslavery people hunted me down like a wolf. I lost one of my sons there."

When the long night finally ended, Brown and his men looked out to see marines prepared to attack the engine house with guns, bayonets, and sledgehammers. Beyond the troops, as far as the men could see, spectators watched from sidewalks, streets, and buildings.

But, faced with certain defeat, Brown betrayed no sign of fear or indecision.

Instead, said Colonel Washington, he was "the coolest man I ever saw in defying danger and death. With one son dead by his side, and another shot through, he felt the pulse of his dying son with one hand, and held his rifle with the other, and commanded his men with the utmost composure, encouraging them to be firm, and to sell their lives as dearly as they could."

Again Stuart came to the door and demanded Brown's unconditional surrender, and again Brown refused.

"I prefer to die here," he said.

Stuart jumped aside and waved his cap, the signal to attack. The marines stormed the engine house, spectators cheering wildly as the troops battered at the door with sledgehammers. It refused to yield, however, and they picked up a nearby ladder and used it as a battering ram.

Brown and his men kept up a withering fire, but the door finally shattered and the marines raced in, led by a Major W.W. Russell and Lieutenant Israel Green.

Brown said later he could have killed Russell "as easy as a mosquito, . . . but I supposed he only came in to receive our surrender. There had been loud and long calls of 'surrender' from us. . . ."

A marine fatally bayoneted Dauphin Thompson as he crawled under a fire engine, and Jeremiah Anderson was pinned to the wall with a bayonet while his arms were raised in surrender. Later, as he lay dying on the ground outside, a farmer forced open his mouth, spat tobacco juice into it, and kicked him in the face and body.

Lieutenant Green jumped on top of the engine looking for Brown, who lowered the rifle he held in his hands. When Green saw him, said Daingerfield, the officer "sprang about twelve feet at him, giving

The United States Marines storming the engine house.

an under thrust of his sword, striking Brown about midway the body, and raising him completely from the ground. Brown fell forward . . . while Green struck him several times over the head. . . . It seems that Green's sword, in making the thrust, struck Brown's belt and did not penetrate the body. The sword was bent double. . . ."

The attack was over in minutes.

Brown was carried to the paymaster's room in the armory, while a lynch mob called for his blood.

But he seemed unafraid, said Virginia Governor Henry A. Wise, and looked like "a broken-winged hawk, lying on his back, with a fearless eye, and his talons set for further fight, if need be."

Nine of his men had been killed, Watson was dying, and the rest were captured or fleeing for their lives. A mob threw Oliver's body into a pit, then tossed Newby's body on top, thinking they were insulting Oliver by placing a black man in the same grave. The bodies of Anderson, Leeman, and Taylor were flung into another pit.

The dream Brown had pursued for decades lay in apparent ruin and he was surrounded by enemies. Yet when Colonel Lee asked if he wished to be left alone, he said no, he would gladly answer the questions of his interrogators.

Within hours they were there: Senator James Mason of Virginia, author of the Fugitive Slave Law; Representative Clement L. Vallandingham of Ohio, a strong supporter of slavery; and Matthew Johnson, the United States marshal who had been too afraid to arrest Brown in Cleveland, but now tried to get him to implicate leading abolitionists, including Joshua Giddings, in the attack on Harpers Ferry.

They and many others came to mock and to question. And Brown, who had not slept in over sixty hours, welcomed them because he wanted "to make himself and his motives clearly understood."

But first he pleaded with his captors to take care of the dying Watson, saying: "I will ask for him what I would not ask for myself; let him have kind treatment, for he is as pure and noble-hearted a youth as ever breathed the breath of life."

And then he began to answer their questions.

"In the midst of his enemies," wrote a reporter for the Baltimore *American and Commercial Advertiser*, ". . . with the gallows staring him full in the face, he lay on the floor, and, in reply to every question, gave answers that betokened the spirit that animated him."

He now seemed more comfortable as teacher and preacher than he had as guerrilla leader, and when one man demanded, "Upon what principle do you justify your acts?" Brown replied:

"Upon the Golden Rule. I pity the poor in bondage that have none to help them: that is why I am here; not to gratify any personal animosity, revenge, or vindictive spirit. It is my sympathy with the oppressed and the wronged, that are as good as you and as precious in the sight of God."

Dozens of questions were hurled at him for hour after hour, until finally Brown looked at the men surrounding him and declared: "I wish to say . . . that you had better — all you people of the South — prepare yourselves for a settlement of this question, that must come up for settlement sooner than you are prepared for it. . . . You may dispose of me very easily — I am nearly disposed of now; but this question is still to be settled — this negro question I mean; the end of that is not yet."

CHAPTER TEN

MAKE WAY FOR LIBERTY!

The attack on Harpers Ferry spread panic throughout the South.

Authorities strengthened slave patrols, declared martial law, whipped whites who expressed sympathy for slaves, burned books considered "anti-Southern," and threatened to hang any black man, woman, or child who even *looked* rebellious.

Many slave owners around Harpers Ferry and throughout Virginia hurriedly made plans to sell their slaves farther south, fearing they would be freed by abolitionists or start a rebellion.

In the days following the raid, fearful Virginians bought over ten thousand pistols, and women and children ran "crying and screaming" into churches after hearing rumors of armed slaves gathering in the mountains.

Another rumor spread that thousands of abolitionists were coming down a valley near Harpers Ferry, killing as they came.

"The intelligence from Harpers Ferry," wrote a reporter in the Baltimore *American and Commercial Advertiser*, "has created an excitement in our community and throughout the whole length and breadth of the country that has scarcely been equalled by any preceding occurrence of the present century."

A Richmond newspaper carried an ad offering ten thousand dollars to anyone who captured Joshua Giddings alive and five thousand dollars for his head.

"John Brown did not only capture and hold Harpers Ferry for twenty hours," said Osborne Anderson, "but he held the whole South."

In the hours following Brown's capture, furious mobs talked so much about lynching him and his men that the marines moved them to the county jail in Charlestown, about eight miles from Harpers Ferry.

Although they had attacked federal property and should have been tried in a federal court, Virginia officials announced they would be tried in a state court within a few days.

This action was apparently meant to advance the political career of Governor Wise and strengthen the argument of Southern leaders that their states were independent of federal control.

Southern leaders charged that Brown's raid was part of a Republican Party plot to destroy slavery, and some — like Jefferson Davis, who was now a senator from Mississippi — predicted it was only the first "of those violent proceedings which can only be considered civil war."

Lieutenant Stuart found the carpetbag full of papers at the Kennedy farm, including letters from the Secret Six and several of Brown's friends. Virginia authorities immediately began extradition proceedings against these "collaborators."

Governor Wise said if another attack occurred, Virginia would invade other states if necessary to capture the raiders.

President Buchanan mobilized the power of the Federal Government to track down anyone authorities thought might have been involved in the raid, and United States marshals were soon headed north armed with arrest warrants.

Gerrit Smith burned all his letters involving Brown's plans, then sent his brother-in-law to Ohio and Boston to destroy other documents that might incriminate him. Howe and Stearns fled to Canada, while Sanborn spent two straight nights destroying letters and manuscripts that could implicate him. Then he also fled to Canada.

Of the Secret Six, only Higginson remained openly defiant, scolding Sanborn for cowardice and quickly persuading him to return and join in planning a plot to rescue Brown.

Frederick Douglass, who would soon be charged

by Virginia authorities with "murder, robbery and inciting to servile insurrection in the State of Virginia," was speaking to a large audience in Philadelphia when they received word of the attack on Harpers Ferry.

"The announcement came upon us," he said, "with the startling effect of an earthquake. It was something to make the boldest hold his breath."

Douglass would have been seized almost immediately if a friendly telegraph operator had not delayed delivery of a telegram instructing the city sheriff to arrest him.

The alarmed Douglass hurried home to Rochester, destroyed several papers and letters, then "barely evaded his pursuers" on a desperate flight to Canada and England.

In Jefferson, Ohio, members of the Ashtabula League of Freedom guarded the roads to stop any federal agents who tried to arrest John, Jr. In Maine, the mother of William Leeman went into shock and would be bedridden for eighteen months, unable to speak.

In Nebraska, the Kagi family mourned the idealistic son and brother who had written them less than one month before: "I believe there are better times dawning, to my sight at least. I am not now laboring and waiting without present reward for myself alone; it is for a future reward for mankind, and for you all."

In Warrenton, Virginia, not far from Harpers Ferry, Harriet Newby was hurriedly sold to a slave trader in Louisiana.

And in isolated North Elba, the Brown family finally learned the enormity of their loss from a newspaper that was several days old.

"There was very little 'weeping or wailing' on the part of our brave household," said Annie. "We were most of us struck dumb, horror stricken with a grief too deep and hard to find expression in words or even tears."

Mary became sick, and was quickly followed by Annie and Salmon's wife, Abbie. Seventeen-year-old Martha, Oliver's pregnant widow, nursed them back to health. But soon she would take ill and die, along with the child she carried.

"Other women give money," she said shortly before her death, "but I have given all; my beloved and my life!"

Governor Wise was determined to give Brown and his men a quick trial, then hang them "in double quick time."

Just three days after his capture, Brown wrote letters to Judge Russell in Boston, another judge in Cleveland, and a friend in Springfield, asking for help in obtaining a lawyer.

Without such help, he declared, "neither the facts in our case can come before the world: nor can we have the benefit of such facts upon our trial. Can you or some other good man come in immediately for the sake of the young men prisoners at least?"

But only a week after the raid, before there was time for a reply to his requests, he was taken hand-cuffed into the courthouse. Brown, suffering from his wounds, was manacled to Edwin Coppoc on one

John Brown's last letter to his wife and children, dated November 30, 1859.

side and supported by an armed guard on the other. Aaron Stevens, who shared a cell with Brown, was so weak he had to be held upright by two bailiffs.

The jailers took care to see that Shields Green and John Copeland were handcuffed separately from their white comrades.

The angry mob that jammed the town square was so unruly the judge feared they would break into his courtroom and lynch Brown. Eighty soldiers with fixed bayonets surrounded the prisoners, while other soldiers trained two cannon on the courthouse to prevent any rescue or escape attempts.

Reporters and townspeople packed the courtroom, which was now the focus of a divided nation. In meetings throughout the land, men and women were gathering to praise or condemn Brown and his raid.

"The day of compromise is passed," the Charlestown *Mercury* warned. "The South must control her own destinies or perish."

In a speech in Philadelphia the second day of Brown's trial, Joshua Giddings reminded his listeners of John Quincy Adams's prediction twenty years before: ". . . the day of the deliverance of the slave *must* come; whether in peace or in blood, he could not tell. But whether it come in peace or in blood," he said, "*let it come.*"

Hazlett and Cook would soon be captured and join those about to go on trial, but Owen Brown,

Osborne Anderson, Francis Meriam, Charles Tidd, and Barclay Coppoc made good their escape.

"For days they made their way through the mountains and swamps, a price on their heads, . . ." said John, Jr. ". . . Once, when they lay in a blackberry thicket, two hundred United States cavalry rode by. Following the troops was a small boy on a pony leading a little dog by a string. The dog smelled them, darted into the brambles barking furiously, but the boy jerked the dog back and galloped on. Had the string broken, or the boy followed the dog's lead, they would all have been captured. They had many escapes as narrow as that."

At the preliminary examination on October 25, the justices asked Brown if he had a lawyer, knowing he did not.

"If you seek my blood, you can have it at any moment, without this mockery of a trial, . . ." he replied with scorn. "I beg for . . . nothing but that which conscience gives, or cowardice would drive you to practice. . . ."

The next day, the Grand Jury met and indicted Brown and his men for "conspiracy with slaves for the purpose of insurrection; with treason against the commonwealth of Virginia; and with murder in the first degree."

Copeland, Leary, Coppoc, and Stevens were indicted on the same charges. Judge Richard Parker immediately ordered them to the courthouse to hear the charges read, but Brown refused to leave his cot.

The jailers carried him into court on the cot, where he asked that his trial be delayed "so that I may in some degree recover, and be able at least to listen to my trial, and hear what questions are asked of the citizens, and what their answers are. . . ."

Judge Parker refused and ordered the trial to begin the next morning, with the trials of Stevens, Green, Copeland, and Coppoc to follow.

Thus it was that just one day after the indictments were handed down and ten days after his capture, Brown's trial began while he lay on a cot in full view — not only of the spectators who crowded the courtroom — but of the nation that watched through the eyes of the many reporters.

Such haste outraged many in the North, but it was allowed under Virginia laws aimed at controlling slaves and strictly enforced since Nat Turner's rebellion.

Hundreds of Virginia militiamen were stationed in Charlestown, and no one was allowed to pass through Harpers Ferry — the nearest railroad point — without a pass from Governor Wise or prosecutor Andrew Hunter.

The court assigned Brown two Virginia lawyers, including one whose "words rush from his mouth scarce half made up," said a reporter for the New York *Tribune*. "He speaks sentences abreast. . . . His . . . 'whar' and 'thar' are the least of his offenses."

Just as the trial was beginning, Brown's lawyers introduced a telegram from an editor in Akron, Ohio, saying that insanity was hereditary in the Brown family. The move was an attempt to help Brown escape hanging by having him declared insane and placed in an asylum, but Brown would have none of it.

"I look upon it as a miserable artifice . . . and I view it with contempt more than otherwise," he said, raising up on his cot. ". . . and I reject, so far as I am capable, any attempt to interfere in my behalf on that score."

After Brown was returned to jail on the second day of his trial, a recent law school graduate named George Hoyt arrived from Boston and received permission to visit him. Hoyt managed to slip Brown a note from Sanborn, Higginson, and others proposing a rescue attempt, but Brown rejected the idea.

"I doubt if I ought to encourage any attempt to save my life," he said. "I may be wrong, but I think that my great object will be nearer its accomplishment by my death than by my life."

And to Mary he wrote: "I have been *whiped* as the saying *is,* but am sure I can recover all the lost capital occasioned by that disaster; by only hanging a few moments by the neck; . . . I am dayly & hourly striving to gather up what little I may from the wreck."

The trial lasted three-and-a-half days, with witness after witness testifying for prosecutor Andrew

Hunter: Colonel Washington told how Brown had denounced the killing of Watson while carrying a flag of truce, but even then had made no threats against his prisoners; the trainmen quoted Brown as saying it was not his intention that "blood should be spilled"; other witnesses described the seizure of buildings, the wounding and killing of people, and the involvement of both free and enslaved black men in the attacking army.

Brown listened impassively, usually lying on his back with his eyes closed. Only once did he show

This picture depicts a last moment that some say never happened.

anger, and that was when witness Henry Hunter described how he and a saloonkeeper shot William Thompson and tossed his body into the river.

"I felt it my duty," Hunter declared proudly, "and I have no regrets."

Brown struggled to his feet and asked for a delay in the proceedings, protesting that "nothing like a fair trial is to be given me, as it would seem. I gave the names . . . of the persons I wished to have called as witnesses . . . but it appears that they have not been subpoenaed. . . ."

His request was denied and Brown lay back down on the cot, pulled up the blanket and closed his eyes.

The Virginia lawyers immediately withdrew from the case, and the next day Brown was represented by two lawyers hired by antislavery friends in Boston: Hiram Griswold of Cleveland and Samuel Chilton of Washington.

Griswold, Chilton, and Hoyt met with Brown for several hours, and Hoyt remarked afterwards, "I confess, I did not know which most to admire, the thorough honor and admirable qualities of the brave, old border soldier, or the uncontaminated simplicity of the man."

Neither Brown's honorable qualities, uncontaminated simplicity, or new lawyers made any difference in the final outcome, however.

On Monday afternoon, October 31, the jury deliberated for forty-five minutes, then returned to the courtroom and pronounced Brown guilty.

"Guilty of treason, and conspiring and advising with slaves and others to rebel, and murder in the first degree?" asked the court clerk.

"Yes," the foreman replied.

There was no sound after the verdict was read, said one man, and "Old Brown himself said not even a word, but, as on any previous day, turned to adjust his pallet, and then composedly stretched himself upon it."

That night Brown wrote his "Dear Wife and Children, Every One," telling them he supposed they had "learned before this by the newspapers" about the attack on Harpers Ferry and the deaths of Oliver, Watson, and William and Dauphin Thompson.

"I have since been tried," he went on, "and found guilty of treason, etc., and of murder in the first degree. . . . Under all these terrible calamities, I feel quite cheerful in the assurance that God reigns and will overrule all for his glory and the best possible good. . . . Never forget the poor, nor think anything you bestow on them to be lost to you, even though they may be black as Ebedmelech, the Ethiopian eunuch, who cared for Jeremiah in the pit of the dungeon; or as black as the one to whom Philip preached Christ. . . ."

Two days later, Brown was brought into court and

asked if he had anything to say before sentence was pronounced. He was caught by surprise, since he thought the others would be tried before he was sentenced.

But in the midst of what seemed like total defeat, he began another battle in his long war against slavery.

Struggling to his feet, he replied, "I have, may it please the court, a few words to say."

And then, in a voice described as both gentle and firm, he began a speech Higginson would call "unequalled in the history of American oratory for simplicity and power," and which Ralph Waldo Emerson would compare with Abraham Lincoln's Gettysburg Address.

"In the first place," Brown declared, "I deny everything but what I have all along admitted — the design on my part to free the slaves. . . . I never did intend murder, or treason, or the destruction of property, or to excite or incite slaves to rebellion, or to make insurrection.

". . . had I so interfered in behalf of the rich, the powerful, the intelligent, the so-called great, or in behalf of any of their friends . . . it would have been all right; and every man in this court would have deemed it an act worthy of reward rather than punishment. . . .

"This court acknowledges, as I suppose, the validity of the law of God. . . . That teaches me that all things whatsoever I would that men should do to me,

I should do even so to them. It teaches me, further, to 'remember them that are in bonds, as bound with them.' I endeavored to act up to that instruction. . . . Now, if it is deemed necessary that I should forfeit my life for the furtherance of the ends of justice, and mingle my blood further with the blood of my children and with the blood of millions in this slave country whose rights are disregarded by wicked, cruel, and unjust enactments — I submit; so let it be done! . . ."

When Brown finished, Judge Parker quietly told him he was to be publicly hanged on December 2, just one month away. The following morning, Brown received permission to add the following to the letter he had written Mary and the children three days before:

"P.S. Yesterday, November 2, I was sentenced to be hanged on December 2 next. Do not grieve on my account. I am still quite cheerful. God bless you!"

Then he asked that the letter be addressed to Mrs. John Brown, "for there are some other widow Browns in North Elba."

Higginson informed Mary of the death sentence before the letter reached her, however, and said "the tall, strong woman bent her head for a few minutes . . . then she raised it, and spoke calmly as before."

The trials of Copeland, Green, Coppoc, and Cook went quickly, and all were sentenced to hang

December 16. Prosecutor Hunter was "almost ferocious" in his arguments against Green, said one observer, "whose boldly careless bearing had aroused all the malignity that slave ownership and race prejudice necessarily produced."

But Hunter was so impressed by Copeland's dignity and courage, he said later: "If it had been possible to recommend a pardon for any of them it would have been this man Copeland. . . ."

Judge Parker decided to drop the charge of treason against Copeland and Green, ruling that black people were noncitizens and therefore legally incapable of committing treason.

William J. Watkins, a black abolitionist from New York, said angrily: "It was the climax of tyranny to rob us of the paltry privilege of being traitors to this devil-inspired and God-forsaken government."

Brown received so many visitors that Captain John Avis, his jailer, had to usher them into the cell in groups. Brown talked to everyone who came, and tried especially hard to "faithfully, plainly, and kindly" convert his proslavery visitors.

He was outraged, however, by clergymen who defended slavery, and told one who wanted to kneel in prayer with him, "I would not insult God by bowing down in prayer with anyone who had the blood of a slave on his skirts."

Then Brown began to write letters that helped

change the defeat at Harpers Ferry into the Samson-like victory he had long foreseen. In the first week after his conviction he wrote very few, then suddenly the words began to pour forth from his pen: eloquent words, words thanking God for the opportunity to serve Him; words of hope, love, and joy to his family and friends.

Sheriff James Campbell, who was required to read the letters before mailing them, often had to wipe tears from his eyes.

"I can trust God with both the time and the manner of my death," he wrote Mary and the children on November 8, "believing, as I now do, that for me at this time to seal my testimony for God and humanity with my blood will do vastly more toward advancing the cause I have earnestly endeavored to promote, than all I have done in my life before. I beg of you all meekly and quietly to submit to this. . . . Think, too, of the crushed millions who 'have no comforter.' I charge you all never in your trials to forget the griefs 'of the poor that cry, and of those that have none to help them.' . . ."

"P.S. I cannot remember a night so dark as to have hindered the coming day, nor a storm so furious or dreadful as to prevent the return of warm sunshine and a cloudless sky. . . ."

Newspapers reprinted many of the more than one hundred letters he wrote, and soon his antislavery words were joined by those of others: speeches by Emerson and Thoreau; poems by Walt Whitman, Herman Melville, and John Greenleaf Whittier; hundreds of sermons by ministers throughout the North.

And letters began to pour into Brown's cell in reply.

A Quaker woman from Rhode Island told him that although she and most other Quakers would not think it right to use violence, "we may judge thee a deliverer who wished to release millions from a more cruel oppression. If the American people honor Washington for resisting with bloodshed for seven years an unjust tax, how much more ought thou to be honored for seeking to free the poor slaves."

From Indiana, black writer and antislavery lecturer Frances Ellen Harper wrote: ". . . in the name of the slave mother, her heart rocked to and fro by the agony of her mournful separations — I thank you. . . . You have rocked the bloody Bastille. . . ."

In the midst of his final effort to force the nation to confront the evil of slavery, surrounded by jailers and hundreds of armed soldiers, and with his death less than two weeks away, Brown complained that Mary wasn't telling him about the family's crops.

"Why will you not say to me whether you had any crops mature this season?" he asked. "If so, what ones? Although I may nevermore intermeddle with your worldly affairs, I have not yet lost all interest in them. A little history of your success or of your failures I should very much prize. . . ."

He tried to discourage Mary from coming to see him, out of fear of the treatment she would receive. Judge Russell's wife visited Brown and was the object of so much anger from the inhabitants, Hoyt said, he wondered how she managed to get away unhurt.

And there was "wild, almost unappeasable fury" from the townspeople when a Quaker woman from the North came to nurse Brown and his men.

When he heard that well-known abolitionist and feminist Lydia Maria Child was also planning to visit, Brown was appalled and managed to stop the trip.

"Keep Mrs. Child away at all hazards," Hoyt wrote a friend in Boston. "Brown and his associates will certainly be lynched if she goes there. . . ."

Brown also continued to try and keep Mary from coming, because "it will only cause both of us more sorrow," but she was determined.

"If she comes on here," he wrote on November 8, referring to her in the third person as he often did, "she must be only a gazing-stock throughout the whole journey, to be remarked upon in every look, word, and action. . . . Oh, Mary! do not come, but patiently wait for the meeting of those who love God and their fellow-men, where no separation must follow. . . ."

But Mary began the journey, traveling from North Elba to Philadelphia, where she stayed with William Still and his wife.

At this same time, an unprecedented number of fires broke out in the countryside around Harpers Ferry, consuming barns, stables, haystacks, stock yards, and farm implements.

Night after night, reported the Richmond *Enquirer*, "the heavens are illuminated by the lurid glare of burning property."

Blacks were suspected of setting the fires, especially after the burning of property belonging to three of the jurors who found Brown guilty, including the jury foreman, Walter Shirley. Several horses and sheep belonging to another farmer also died suddenly, as if they had been poisoned.

"There is now here a source of much disquietude to me," Brown wrote Mary on November 21, still trying to stop her, "namely, the fires which are almost of daily and nightly occurrence in this immediate neighborhood. . . . I know . . . [that] we shall be charged with them. . . . In the existing state of public feeling I can easily see a further objection to your coming here at present; but I did not intend saying another word to you on that subject."

Mary reached Harpers Ferry on November 30, the same day Colonel Lee — acting on President Buchanan's orders — arrived with two hundred fifty soldiers to guard against a rumored Northern invasion.

It was almost 3:30 P.M. the next day, when Captain Avis opened Brown's door and let her in the cell. Brown and Mary embraced and cried, then sat down together for the last time. They talked alone for several hours, then had dinner with Captain Avis and his family.

Governor Wise had ordered Mary to return to Harpers Ferry that night, and the hour soon came for her to leave. For the first time, Brown lost his composure and angrily asked why Mary couldn't spend this final night with him. But his anger quickly passed and he and Mary embraced for the last time.

They wept and prayed, then she was gone.

Brown rose at dawn on the day of his execution. He read the Bible, marking several passages that had held special meaning for him, then sent for Andrew Hunter to come and write his will.

Hunter told him he could write the will himself, but Brown replied, "Yes, but I am so busy now answering my correspondence of yesterday, and this being the day of my execution, I haven't time. . . ."

Brown bequeathed several items to his family, including his surveyor's compass, which he gave to John, Jr., and "my large, old Bible, containing the family record," which he gave to Ruth. He also left fifty dollars toward his debt to the New England Woolen Company, still troubled by his decades-long obligation.

"This all occurred a short time before the officers

came to take Brown out to execution," Hunter said, ". . . while I was drawing the will he was answering letters with a cool and steady hand. . . ."

And then it was time.

Captain Avis and a guard unlocked his cell, and Brown walked out. He gave his silver watch to Avis and his Bible to the guard because of their kindness toward him.

Proceeding down the corridor, he stopped before the cell of Copeland and Green, and told them, "Stand up like men, and do not betray your friends."

He gave each man a twenty-five-cent piece, telling them it was a keepsake from him, then said good-bye to Cook, Coppoc, and Stevens.

Avis and the guard led him down the corridor and into the street. As he stepped outside, Brown handed guard Hiram O'Bannon a note he had written that morning.

It read: "I, John Brown am now quite *certain* that the crimes of this *guilty land*: will never be purged *away*; but with Blood. I had *as I now think: vainly* flattered myself that without *very much* bloodshed; it might be done."

While Brown was preparing to ride to the scaffold, crowds gathered at special services throughout the North. "Martyr Day," they called the day of Brown's execution. In Boston, all black business places were closed and draped in mourning cloth.

In cities, towns, and villages, men and women wore

crepe armbands decorated with pictures of Brown. In Lowell, Massachusetts, a black man mounted a bell on a cart and walked slowly through the streets, tolling the bell as he went.

In Cambridge, poet Henry Wadsworth Longfellow predicted that Brown's death would mark "the date of a new Revolution, quite as much needed as the old one. Even now as I write, they are leading Old John Brown to execution in Virginia for attempting to rescue slaves! This is sowing the wind to reap the whirlwind, which will come soon."

Brown, his hands bound, was helped into the undertaker's open wagon. The undertaker was seated on the coffin in the middle of the wagon, and Brown sat down beside him.

"Captain Brown," the undertaker said, "you are in better spirits to-day than I."

"I have good cause to be," Brown replied.

The scaffold was on the high part of a plowed field at the edge of town, and just beyond the field the land began to dip into a valley. In the distance, the Shenandoah River shone in the sun and a soft haze covered the Blue Ridge Mountains.

"This is a beautiful country," Brown said, walking toward the scaffold and gazing at the vista that stretched for thirty miles. "I have never had the pleasure of seeing it before."

Fifteen hundred calvary and militia formed a huge square around the scaffold and cannon were trained

John Brown seated on his coffin on the way to his execution.

on it. One of the militiamen looking on approvingly was a young actor named John Wilkes Booth, who thought abolitionists were "the *only* traitors in the land."

Brown walked quickly up the scaffold, as though he were "a willing assistant, instead of the victim."

Sheriff Campbell placed a hood over his head, then led him to the trapdoor and put the noose around his neck.

"I hope they will not keep me standing here any longer than necessary," Brown told him.

But there was so much confusion among the soldiers over their assigned positions that Brown was kept waiting about ten minutes.

All the while, said Hunter, who watched from a few feet away, "he was as cool and as firm as any human being I ever saw under such circumstances."

Suddenly the trapdoor crashed open and Brown's body plunged through. In a split second the rope jerked to a halt and he hung convulsing against the noonday sky.

"So perish all such enemies of Virginia!" cried Colonel J.T.L. Preston of the Virginia Military Institute. "All such enemies of the Union! All such foes of the human race!"

In late afternoon the body was shipped to Harpers Ferry, and Brown began his final journey to North Elba in a procession watched by the nation.

The train passed through Baltimore and Philadelphia, where large crowds gathered. Wendell Phillips joined Mary in New York City to help escort the body north.

In Troy, New York, Mary was described as "quite unwell," "unable to see anyone," and "almost entirely prostrated," but after stopping overnight, she was able to continue.

In Rutland and Vegennes, Vermont, and in every town they passed through, crowds gathered in the streets and church bells tolled as the train rolled by. Finally, after four days, they crossed Lake Champlain and traveled to Elizabethtown, where Brown's body was placed in the courthouse. There an honor guard of local men stood guard over him till dawn.

And then it was time for the final miles — the journey through the mountains he loved so well to the home he once dreamed of living in for the rest of his life.

They reached the farm on December 7 as darkness was settling over Whiteface, and Mary greeted Ruth, Annie, Sarah, and little Ellen with "a burst of love and anguish."

The body was placed in the main room of the still-unpainted house and neighbors came to pay homage. Then the next day Phillips gave a eulogy to "the marvelous old man."

"History will date Virginia Emancipation from Harpers Ferry," he declared. "True, the slave is still there. So, when the tempest uproots a pine . . . it looks green for months — a year or two. John Brown has loosened the roots of the slave system; it only breathes — it does not live, hereafter. . . ."

Lyman Epps led his sons in the hymn their friend and neighbor had sung with them so often:

> "Blow ye the trumpet, blow
> Sweet is Thy work, my God, my King. . . .
> Why should we start, and fear to die.
> With songs and honors sounding loud.
> Ah, lovely appearance of death."

"The singing was done by colored people chiefly," Ruth said, and it seemed "as though my dear father was with us in spirit and joined in the chorus of his favorite hymn. . . ."

The coffin was carried outside and lowered into the earth beside a great boulder that bore the name of Brown's freedom-loving Revolutionary War ancestor, Captain John Brown; and Frederick, "murdered at Osawatomie for his adherence to the cause of freedom."

Brown had heard Kagi talk about the great Swiss

The boulder near John Brown's grave in North Elba, New York.

patriot, Arnold Winkelreid, who cried, "Make way for Liberty!" as he sacrificed his life on the enemy's spears to clear a path for his comrades.

Now the lives of Brown, Kagi, and their comrades had been sacrificed to make way for liberty: a liberty that had haunted Brown since the day over forty years before when he saw the black boy beaten and asked of him and all those who suffered in slavery: "Is not God their father?"

"There is no seed that comes to so swift and abundant a harvest as the blood of martyrs spilled upon the ground," Brown told John, Jr., shortly before going down to Harpers Ferry.

Now Brown's blood had been spilled, and the harvest of freedom he envisioned would soon begin with the coming of the Civil War.

"He sleeps in the blessings of the crushed and the poor," Phillips said, as Mary and her daughters wept, "and men believe more firmly in virtue, now that such a man has lived."

EPILOGUE

"They could kill him, but they could not answer him."

Frederick Douglass

John Brown's tiny army struck terror into the heart of the South, showed how fragile the system of slavery was beneath its brutal exterior, and accelerated the division between North and South that would explode into the Civil War less than two years later.

"A house divided against itself cannot stand," Abraham Lincoln had declared in 1858 in his first debate with Stephen Douglas. "I believe that this Government cannot endure permanently half slave and half free. . . ."

After being elected president, however, Lincoln refused to enforce a law that called for giving freedom to the slaves of anyone fighting against the Union.

"If I could save the Union without freeing any slave," he responded to abolitionist critics in 1862, "I would do it; and if I could save it by freeing all the slaves, I would do it; and if I could do it by freeing some and leaving others alone, I would also do that. What I do about Slavery and the colored race, I do because it helps to save this Union. . . ."

But the Civil War that John Brown had foreseen and helped bring about, finally forced Lincoln and other leaders to turn from compromising with slavery to ending it.

"Like Samson," Frederick Douglass predicted shortly before Brown's execution, "he has laid his hands upon the pillars of this great national temple of cruelty and blood, and when he falls, that temple will speedily crumble to its final doom, burying its denizens in its ruins."

The story of John Brown and his fight against slavery is thus as much the story of a nation and a time as of a man.

"He headed no party, changed no law, won no large following, suffered an ignominious death," John, Jr., said of his father's long and often lonely struggle against slavery. "His life went out in tragic gloom and apparent failure. But suddenly he seemed to be, as Thoreau said, 'more alive than any man living.' There was something like public remorse and

shame that a great nation should have shirked its duty,
[and] allowed one old man to hurl himself to death
against a national wrong."

Forty years after the attack on Harpers Ferry, the
bodies of eight of John Brown's comrades — including Newby and Leary — were disinterred from their
crude graves on the bank of the Shenandoah and
brought to North Elba to be buried with their leader.
The bodies of Aaron Stevens and Albert Hazlett were
also disinterred from their graves in New Jersey and
brought to the farm.

Lewis Leary's widow, who as a young bride had
kissed him good-bye on that long-ago morning in
Oberlin, Ohio, now lived in Lawrence, Kansas, and
was unable to attend the ceremonies. She still trea-
sured Leary's bloodstained cape, and she still revered
the cause for which he died.

"I am a widow and old and alone," she wrote to
one of the organizers, "but I rejoice to know that the
hero of Osawatomie and his followers are not forgotten. I remember them with pride and their brave
struggle for the liberty of an oppressed race."

On a warm day in August, 1899, fifteen hundred
spectators gathered near the gravesite alongside the
granite boulder, while Lyman Epps — now an elderly man — once more led his sons in singing
Brown's favorite hymns.

It had been sixty-two years since John Brown
stood in the back of the Congregational Church in

Hudson, raised his right hand and declared: "Here, before God, in the presence of these witnesses, I consecrate my life to the destruction of slavery."

Now slavery had been destroyed and Brown, with his all-consuming hatred of "the crime of crimes" and "abomination of abominations," was one of the reasons why.

"Until this blow was struck," Frederick Douglass said of the attack on Harpers Ferry, "the prospect for Freedom was dim, shadowy, and uncertain. The irrepressible conflict was one of words, votes, and compromises. When John Brown stretched forth his arm the sky was cleared — the time for compromise was gone — the armed hosts stood face to face over the chasm of a broken Union and the clash of arms was at hand!"

BIBLIOGRAPHY

GOVERNMENT PUBLICATIONS:

Calendar of Virginia State Papers, Jan. 1, 1836–Apr. 15, 1869. Vol. XI. Richmond: H.W. Flurnoy, Secretary of the Commonwealth and State Library, 1893. Contains many of the letters found in John Brown's carpetbag, including Harriet Newby's letters to her husband, Dangerfield Newby. pp. 310–11.

BOOKS:

Abels, Jules. *Man on Fire: John Brown and the Cause of Liberty.* New York: Macmillan Co., 1971.

Anderson, Osborne Perry. *A Voice From Harpers Ferry.* Boston: Printed for the Author, 1861.

Aptheker, Herbert. *Abolitionism: A Revolutionary Movement.* Boston: Twayne Publishers, division of G.K. Hall, 1989.

―――. *Nat Turner's Slave Rebellion.* New York: Humanities Press, Inc., 1966.

―――. *A Documentary History of the Negro People in the United States, Vol. 1: From the Colonial Times Through the Civil War.* New York: Citadel Press, 1951.

Bennett, Lerone, Jr. *Pioneers in Protest.* Chicago: Johnson Publishing Company, 1968.

Boyer, Richard O. *The Legend of John Brown: A Biography and a History.* New York: Alfred A. Knopf, 1973.

Cheek, William F. *Black Resistance Before the Civil War.* Beverly Hills: Glencoe Press, a div. of Macmillan, 1970.

Douglass, Frederick. *Life and Times of Frederick Douglass.* New York: Bonanza Books, 1962.

DuBois, W.E. Burghardt. *John Brown.* New York: International Publishers, 1987.

Gutman, Herbert G., ed. *Who Built America? Working People & The Nation's Economy, Politics, Culture & Society,* Vol. 1. New York: Pantheon Books, 1989.

Hinton, Richard. *John Brown and His Men.* New York: Arno Press and *The New York Times,* 1968.

Hawke, David Freeman, ed. *Herndon's Lincoln: The True Story of a Great Life.* New York: Bobbs-Merrill, 1970.

Katz, William Loren. *Breaking the Chains: African-American Slave Resistance.* New York: Atheneum, 1990.

———. *Eyewitness: The Negro in American History.* New York: Pitman Publishing Corp., 1974.

Kemble, Frances Anne. *Journal of a Residence on a Georgian Plantation in 1838–1839.* Chicago: Afro-Am Press, Chicago). 1969. (Orig. publi. by Harper & Brothers, 1864).

Lerner, Gerda, ed. *Black Women in White America: A Documentary History.* New York: Vintage Books, 1973.

Loewen, James W. *Lies My Teacher Told Me: Everything Your American History Textbook Got Wrong.* New York: The New Press, 1995.

McManus, Edgar J. *Black Bondage in the North.* Syracuse: Syracuse University Press, 1973.

Mullane, Deirdre, ed. *Crossing the Danger Water: Three Hundred Years of African-American Writing.* New York: Anchor/Doubleday, 1993.

Nevins, Allan, ed. *The Diary of John Quincy Adams, 1794–1845.* New York: Frederick Ungar Publ. Co., 1951. Reprint in the American Classics Series, 1969.

Nelson, Truman. *The Old Man: John Brown at Harpers Ferry.* New York: Holt, Rinehart and Winston, 1973.

Oates, Stephen B. *To Purge This Land With Blood: A Biography of John Brown.* Amherst, University of Massachusetts Press, 1984.

Quarles, Benjamin. *Allies for Freedom: Blacks & John Brown*. New York: Oxford University Press, 1974.

———. *Frederick Douglass*. New York: Atheneum, 1968.

Ruchames, Louis, ed. *A John Brown Reader: The Story of John Brown in His Own Words, In the Words of Those Who Knew Him, And In the Poetry and Prose of the Literary Heritage*. New York: Abelard-Schuman, 1959.

Sanborn, Franklin B., ed. *The Life and Letters of John Brown: Liberator of Kansas, and Martyr of Virginia*. Concord: F.B. Sanborn, 1917. (Reissued by the Negro University Press, New York, 1969).

Scott, John Anthony & Scott, Robert Alan. *John Brown of Harpers Ferry*. New York: Facts on File, 1993.

Stampp, Kenneth M. *The Peculiar Institution: Slavery in the Ante-Bellum South*. New York: Alfred A. Knopf, 1956.

Stavis, Barrie. *John Brown: The Sword and the Word*. Cranbury: A.S. Barnes and Co., Inc., 1970.

Sterling, Dorothy, ed. *Speak Out in Thunder Tones: Letters and Other Writings by Black Northerners, 1787– 1865*. Garden City: Doubleday, 1973.

Still, William. *The Underground Railroad*. New York: Arno Press and *The New York Times*, 1968.

Zinn, Howard. *A People's History of the United States, 1492–Present* (Harper Perennial, New York). 1995.

PERIODICALS:

Atkinson, Eleanor. "The Soul of John Brown: Recollections of the Great Abolitionist by his Son." *The American Magazine* (October, 1909). pp. 633–643.

Brown, John, Jr. "John Brown's Family Compact." *The Nation* (December 25, 1890). p. 500.

Cotter, Jr. Edward N. "John Brown in the Adirondacks." *Adirondack Life* (Summer, 1972). pp. 8–12.

Dana, Jr., R.H. "How We Met John Brown." *The Atlantic Monthly*, Vol. XXVIII, No. CLXV (July, 1871). pp. 1–9.

Fletcher, Robert S. "John Brown and Oberlin." *The Oberlin Alumni Magazine* (February, 1932). pp. 135– 141.

Land, Mary. "John Brown's Ohio Environment." *The Ohio State Archaeological and Historical Quarterly* (January, 1948). pp. 24–47.

Levy, Leonard W. "Sims' Case: The Fugitive Slave Law in Boston in 1851." *Journal of Negro History,* (January, 1950). pp. 39–74.

Love, Rose Leary. "A Few Facts About Lewis Sheridan Leary Who Was Killed at Harpers Ferry in John Brown's Raid." *Negro History Bulletin* (June, 1943). pp. 198, 215.

———. "The Five Brave Negroes With John Brown at Harpers Ferry." *Negro History Bulletin* (April, 1964). pp. 164–169.

Pease, Jane H. and William H. "Ends, Means, and Attitudes: Black-White Conflict in the Antislavery Movement." *Civil War History* (June, 1972). pp. 117– 128.

Sanborn, Franklin H. "The Virginia Campaign of John Brown." *The Atlantic Monthly* (February, 1875). pp. 224–233.

———. "The Virginia Campaign of John Brown." *The Atlantic Monthly* (May, 1875). pp. 591–600.

Shaw, Albert. "John Brown in the Adirondacks." *Review of Reviews* (September, 1896). pp. 311–317.

NEWSPAPERS:

Anonymous. "American Civilization Illustrated: A Great Slave Auction. 400 Men, Women and Children Sold." *The New York Daily Tribune,* March 9, 1859. p. 5.

———. "The Virginia Rebellion." *The New York Times,* October 29, 1859. p 1.

———. "The Virginia Rebellion." *The New York Times,* October 31, 1859. p. 1.

INDEX